Praise for *Becoming Your Best*

"We found *Becoming Your Best* to be extremely effective for our group. They use a fast-paced interactive approach which brings great energy into the room. The program used content based on research, which is proven and successful which led to greater buy in from the group. Further, the content was appropriate and applicable making the time and energy well spent."

—Jerry Jones Jr., Dallas Cowboys

"I have a few books on my shelves that have deepened my appreciation of profound principles of life. I have many that articulate strategies and tools that lead to greater results in many domains. But I own precious few that excel at both. Shallenberger not only invites careful thought about first principles, but offers generous wisdom from a lifetime of experience to make them live in your life. This is not a book to read. It is a book to live."

—Joseph Grenny, coauthor of *Crucial Conversations: Tools for Talking When Stakes Are High* and *Influencer: The New Science of Leading Change*

"If you're motivated to improve, don't put down this book until you've read every page. Whatever your profession or background, *Becoming Your Best* provides a masterful approach. It's filled with real-life, inspirational stories as well as powerful tools that an individual, family, or organization can immediately implement."

—Jack Canfield, coauthor of *The Success Principles* and *Chicken Soup for the Soul*

"Steve Shallenberger has been an inspiring leader in several companies and three different industries, while at the same time being highly sought after as a guide to others through their own business and personal development. *Becoming Your Best* is the distillation of that lifetime of experience into a set of clear, timeless principles from which all of us can learn how to develop and sustain excellence. It's the most valuable time you will spend with a book this year!"

—**Randal Quarles,** Managing Director, the Carlyle Group
and former Under Secretary of the U.S. Treasury

"Steve Shallenberger is a positive influence on everyone he meets. He's distilled the principles that have steered his own life into *Becoming Your Best.*"

—**Richard and Linda Eyre,** *New York Times* bestselling
authors of *The Entitlement Trap* and *Teaching Children Values*

"In *Becoming Your Best,* Steve Shallenberger masterfully teaches how to blend all of the variables that you control with eternal principles of success. He also helps people to see that they can control vastly more variables than they would ever have believed. I believe this book will positively change who you become. It will make you more successful in any pursuit, but, more important, it will help turn you into the person you might otherwise only dream of becoming."

—**Blake Roney,** Founder and Chairman, Nu Skin

"I can say with confidence that the principles taught in this groundbreaking book will provide you with a foolproof road map on how to excel in life. Whether you're interested in becoming the best CEO, coach, athlete, spouse, or parent or becoming the best in your career, you need look no further than applying what is taught in *Becoming Your Best.*"

—**Dallin Larsen,** Founder and Chairman, MonaVie

"*Becoming Your Best* is a fun and inspiring book to read. It provides simple yet compelling strategies for dramatically improving your effectiveness, level of accomplishment, and personal satisfaction in the way you go about doing it. I highly recommend this book for corporate leaders."

—**Bob Marquardt,** President, Management & Training Corporation

"A fascinating book on understanding and improving one's personal balance, one's relationships, and one's leadership and management success. I wish I could have had this book when I started my Air Force career in 1970. Steve Shallenberger's research, timeless stories, and delightful writing style make this a book you'll want to refer to for the rest of your life—I know I will! Enjoy."

—Gregory "Speedy" Martin, General, USAF (Retired)

"A must read for anyone looking to lead themselves and others through a transformation of success in life, family, and business. This is one of those books that I will pass down to my son in hopes that he will adapt Steve's 12 guiding constants for becoming your best. Required reading for anyone who strives for excellence."

—James D. Murphy, author of *Flawless Execution* and Founder/CEO, Afterburner, Inc.

"I've worked with thousands of speakers who have amazing ideas. Steve and his team have developed something powerful in *Becoming Your Best*. Every person, family, or organization needs to attend a live Becoming Your Best event and read this book. It's a game changer!"

—James Malinchak, featured on ABC's hit TV show, *Secret Millionaire*, founder, www.BigMoneySpeaker.com

"For the past eighteen years, I have hired hundreds of speakers. Over the years, one speakers message runs into the next and the thrill of hearing speakers' presentations and messages has dulled. Yet when I read and listened to Steve Shallenberger' s Becoming Your Best, I knew he was different and that I had to hire him and bring his message to my YPO client - Global One. It was unique, different than any other message, and extremely inspiring and actionable! Everyone needs to hear this message."

Samantha Borland, YPO Global One Chapter Director

"*Becoming Your Best* is a powerful and simple approach. The unique approach taught in this book can be used by an executive, individual, family, or organization."

—Anson Dorrance, Women's Soccer Coach, North Carolina, 22-time Collegiate National Champion

Becoming Your

Best

Becoming Your

Best

THE 12 PRINCIPLES OF
HIGHLY SUCCESSFUL
LEADERS

STEVEN R. SHALLENBERGER

Mc
Graw
Hill
Education

New York   Chicago   San Francisco   Athens   London   Madrid
Mexico City   Milan   New Delhi   Singapore   Sydney   Toronto

2 3 4 5 6 7 8 9   LCR   24 23 22 21 20

ISBN   978-0-07-183998-3
MHID   0-07-183998-4

e-ISBN 978-0-07-183999-0
e-MHID   0-07-183999-2

Library of Congress Cataloging-in-Publication Data

Shallenberger, Steven R.
    Becoming your best : the 12 principles of highly successful leaders / Steven R. Shallenberger. — 1 Edition.
        pages cm
        ISBN 978-0-07-183998-3 (hardback) — ISBN 0-07-183998-4 1. Leadership.
    I. Title.
    HD57.7.S4747 2014
    658.4′092—dc23   2014029562

McGraw-Hill Education books are available at special quantity discounts to use as premiums and sales promotions or for use in corporate training programs. To contact a representative, please visit the Contact Us pages at www.mhprofessional.com.

To my extraordinary wife, Roxanne

Contents

Foreword

Some books stand out like a beacon in a storm. Such books help you realize that as you focus on the things that you can control, you emerge a stronger and more capable person, you develop stronger and healthier relationships, and you can create a higher-trust culture of excellence in your organization. Such books can also be powerful catalysts for helping you make major breakthroughs in your effectiveness and in reaching your fullest potential, whether individually or as a team.

Becoming Your Best is just such a book.

I've found that the 12 principles taught in this wonderful book are crucial to the success of any leader, in any organization and in any industry. Not only that, but these are the very same principles that lead to being a successful parent and developing long-lasting relationships that withstand the storms of life. In an increasingly low-trust world, more than ever before, we need principle-centered individuals who know how to build enduring relationships and who demonstrate strong leadership capabilities—whether in leading themselves or in leading others. *Becoming Your Best* will help you become one of these people.

I have known and watched Steven Shallenberger for more than 30 years. He is someone who has been "in the arena"—that is, he's a doer and a practitioner. He has built and run multiple businesses, and he has led numerous organizations and thousands of people. Some of the best experiences of my life were when he and I worked side by side for several years at the Covey Leadership Center, helping to build that organization around the world. Along the way, I've witnessed his leadership up close and personal, and I've emerged from all these many experiences with this clear conviction: Steve is as good a person as I have known. He is who you hope he is. He models the principles that he teaches here. He's a principle-centered individual who has touched tens of thousands of lives for good in many different companies and industries. In other words, he practices what he teaches—he puts to work in his own life the principles he espouses here.

There are many reasons that I love this book. Let me share three of them.

First, this book focuses on universal and timeless *principles*. Principles, as contrasted with practices, apply and work across countries, cultures, and situations. As a result, this is not a flavor-of-the-month type of book. It contains proven, time-tested principles for how to achieve your fullest potential, how to create innovative and imaginative solutions, and how to find peace and balance in a chaotic and turbulent world. I've personally seen the power of the principles that Steve teaches as I've traveled and met with hundreds of organizations in more than 40 countries over the last several years. In my book *The Speed of Trust*, I discuss the importance of specific actions—behaviors—that are based on principles and that lead to high-trust relationships. I've witnessed firsthand how the principles discussed in *Becoming Your Best* directly contribute to high-trust relationships and how that foundation of trust ultimately defines successful people and organizations.

Second, consistent with Steve's being a practitioner, this book is intensely *practical*. It deals with opportunities, challenges, and threats at the street level. It is not a hypothetical book; rather, it is a book that is full of tools and inspirational examples of how to work through real-life situations as you make your good better and your better best. This approach takes us from *knowing* into *doing*. As the saying goes, "To know and not to do is not to know." The pragmatic richness of this engaging book takes us from mere knowing and gives us a path into real doing—into deep application.

Third, this book *inspires*. It is simultaneously inspirational and aspirational. I am deeply impressed with Steve's approach because he reminds us that the best still lies in front of us—individually, for a family, and for a business—and that each of us can achieve the best that is within us. *Becoming Your Best* teaches us how to recognize and think through the obstacles that prevent us from realizing our dreams, hopes, and desires. It clearly shows us how to turn those obstacles into a proactive plan for achieving a sustainable positive result. Applying the principles in this book not only gives us hope, but will lead to the realization of our hopes.

Put another way, *Becoming Your Best* gives us a new lens, an entirely new way of seeing and thinking that can change our lives and our organizations in a positive way. It is a book of possibilities and hope for all, regardless of age, nationality, or circumstances. It is a book of encouragement, vision, and solutions.

Regardless of your title or position—whether you are a president, parent, coach, leader/manager, administrator, technician, mechanic, professional, farmer, civil servant, soldier, teacher, team member, employee, or leader of a country—*Becoming Your Best* will inspire you and lead you to greater heights.

Steve has been a great friend, mentor, and trusted advisor to me for more than 30 years. As I travel and conduct my work around the world, I've personally seen how the principles that he illuminates in this insightful book have had a profound impact on people and organizations. Those who make these principles a part of their lives and culture tend to rise to the top. Those who violate these principles tend to break down—and this typically leads to failure.

I highly recommend this book to people, leaders, and organizations everywhere. The path to becoming your best is always a journey, not just a destination. And the key is to enjoy the journey along the way to the destination. Indeed, as the great author Miguel de Cervantes said, "The journey is better than the inn."

Above all, I wish you joy in the journey on the exciting path of becoming your best.

—Stephen M. R. Covey, author of *The Speed of Trust* and coauthor of *Smart Trust*

Acknowledgments

I am forever indebted to the remarkable mentors and advisors who have deeply touched my life: Cal Clark, David Conger, Stephen R. Covey, Robert K. Dellenbach, William N. Jones, Thomas S. Monson, Gardner H. Russell, Lael J. Woodbury, and all of those who have had a powerful influence for good. May I pass it along!

To David C. Clark, my business partner, who has always been encouraging and supportive. To my extraordinary friends at Synergy Companies: *you* are among the best! I appreciate the years of experience with my friends at Eagle Systems International and Covey Leadership. You continue to change the world for good.

To my Harvard CAN Group and the Young Presidents'– World Presidents' Organization forum members, friends, and associates. The Inklings—an incredible group! Thank you for your invaluable perspectives and recommendations.

To my friends and associates at the utility companies and in the energy services industry, who continue to work on world-class service.

I am grateful for my family and extended family members (Humpherys, Quarles, and Shallenbergers), including my ancestors, grandparents, and parents. Thanks, Mom!

I will be forever grateful for the encouragement, brain trust, and writing ideas of my friend John Wilkinson. Without John's help, I might not have been able to launch my thoughts into a book.

To Rob, Dave, Steven, Tom, Daniel, Anne, and their spouses! Rob, thanks for your wise counsel and tireless drive. To each of the children, and Roxanne—you have had such a huge impact on my life.

I appreciate the creative talent and dedicated efforts of Barbara Quittner. Also, to the scores of individuals who reviewed the manuscript and offered valuable recommendations and encouragement, including but not limited to Rick and Linda Eyre, Kathy Clayton, Jerry Johnson, Barry Rellaford, Natalie Anderson, Erin Bakke, Karilyn Turley, Stephen M. R. Covey, Winn Egan, Wynn Hemmert, Kathy Jenkins, Greg Link, Steven McCarty, David Wayt, and Ben Welch.

To Joseph Grenny, Rebecca Merrill, and Kevin Small, for their seasoned advice. Hats off to my fabulous agents at Dupree/ Miller, Jan Miller and Nena Madonia, for their support, encouragement, and expert advice. To Mary Glenn, Thomas W. Miller, Daina Penikas and the talented team at McGraw-Hill: thank you for your enthusiasm, insights, years of experience, reassurance, and laser-like focus.

Introduction

Years ago, when I was fresh out of college, I managed 300 employees, and I wanted to find ways to inspire and lead them. I started looking for common factors that could be found in accomplished people and industry-leading organizations. I thought to myself, if there was a common denominator for success and if I could teach it to our employees, what would that do for our company? This question started me on a journey of research to identify the factors or traits that set apart peak-performing people, leaders, and organizations.

After 40 years of intensive research, my team and I have identified a common denominator for success. This is a set of traits and factors found over and over in high-achieving people and organizations. These are the principles that are embodied by accomplished leaders. I've narrowed down that list to 12 of the most critical factors. I commonly refer to these principles as *guiding constants* because they will consistently guide you and your team to a better place, and because they are constant—they transcend culture and time, and they are especially needed in a rapidly changing world.

In the process of identifying the 12 principles, I came across many types of people. I found that many of those who had the outward appearance of success were often struggling with an inner desire to achieve a greater sense of personal peace, accomplishment, and meaning, and also to maintain happy and productive relationships.

I was initially surprised by some of the comments I received from successful people, until it became apparent that we all have our own challenges and struggles. I began to realize that challenges come in every shape and size, yet they are part of the shared human experience. Do any of these real comments from people I've associated with sound familiar?

- How do I improve communication and accountability, both personally and professionally?

- E-mails, telephone calls, messages, high-pressure projects with deadlines now, and absolutely no end in sight. How do I manage it all?

- A CEO said: I just had the best year ever in our company, but I got divorced during the year. Was my best year ever in business really worth the cost in terms of what happened in my personal life?

- Our company has been number one in our industry for years. How do we avoid complacency and stay number one?

- I feel that I can contribute more at work—I feel underemployed. How can I become one of the most valued employees and feel that I am giving my best, regardless of the circumstances I feel that I am in?

- I have a strained relationship with my wife and children—I don't even talk with one of my sons anymore. How can I restore these important relationships?

- I am addicted to prescription drugs. I am buying prescriptive drugs under the table illegally. Nobody really knows. I am not the person I used to be.

- How do we defend against disruptive threats and develop opportunities in a rapidly changing world?

Maybe you can relate to one or two of these circumstances, or maybe you have someone close to you who is dealing with one of these situations. The promise of this book is that it will give you and your team hope, encouragement, and a positive pathway for resolving issues like these. We've designed a blueprint for building a culture of excellence. This isn't another flavor-of-the-month self-help program. This blueprint is designed to help you and your team to realize sustainable excellence.

Becoming Your Best is not about comparing yourself to another person. It is about becoming your best!

Think about this: out there in the world, there are those who are trying to figure out how to put you out of business or do what you do better than you are doing it; in other words, they're coming up with a "disruptive" technology or service. We've found that those who live by the guiding constants create a culture of excellence in their organizations. This culture of excellence allows those people and businesses to be disruptive in a competitive business world rather than being disrupted and rendered irrelevant.

The Guiding Constants—the 12 Principles of Highly Successful Leaders

For centuries, mariners and explorers have relied on the heavens for navigation because the stars never change their position. For thousands of years, Polaris, or the North Star (see Figure I.1) has

FIGURE I.1 **The North Star**

been available, unmoving and constant, to anyone who looked to it. Those who know how can still use it to find their way.

Just as countless people throughout history have understood key principles and used the appropriate tools to achieve extraordinary results—in flight, medicine, communication, electricity, engineering, and sports, to name a few areas—so each of us can come to understand the key principles that bring about success in life. The laws that affect your success in life are just as timeless, universal, and dependable as the North Star. They work over and over and over!

This is why I chose the term *guiding constants* for these principles: because they are as constant as the stars in the heavens. When you understand and master these constants and use the associated processes and tools effectively, you will achieve significant results on your journey to become your best. You'll see a significant transformation begin to take place in your teams and throughout your organizations as these principles become part of the culture.

Why is it that certain individuals, teams, relationships, organizations, communities, and even countries falter and fail while others persevere and prosper? What makes the difference? What leads some to high levels of performance while others struggle at the opposite end?

I believe that the 12 principles truly make the difference. Sustainable health, happiness, and prosperity stem from mastery of these principles of highly successful leaders. The flow of materials in this book is designed to help you master each one of them, both individually and in your organization. The book is divided into three parts that build on what I consider to be some of the most important areas of our lives.

In Part One, I'll discuss the principles of transformational leadership and management—character, vision, plan, and prioritizing your time.

In Part Two, I'll review the principles of transformational teams and relationships—kindness, trust, communication, and imagination.

And in Part Three, I'll share the keys to transformational living—the principles of accountability, knowledge, peace and balance, and persistence.

The Becoming Your Best Blueprint: How to Apply the 12 Principles

In order to achieve sustainable excellence, you need the right culture to support your strategy. So, how do you create a culture of excellence and develop the right strategy? I've been asked that question repeatedly by leaders, and also another very important question: "How can I make this sustainable for my company so that it's not just a flavor of the month? A lot of training companies have good material, but it's tough to implement. How do we implement this?"

To answer both of those questions, we've created the Becoming Your Best blueprint. This blueprint is results-based and is designed to help you, your family, or your organization implement the 12 principles. It involves simply focusing on one principle a week, personally or as a team, then taking a week to reflect on the results. Do this for 13 weeks, then start over and repeat the process (13 × 4 = 52 weeks). In other words, by focusing on just one principle a week, you'll go through the whole cycle four times a year.

Individually or as a team member or leader, you can focus on one principle each week and ask the question: How can I—or how can we as a team—improve in this area this week? Once you've finished going through each of the 12 principles, spend the thirteenth week reflecting on the lessons you have learned and how and where you have changed. Then, go back and start on the first principle again, this time with an expanded and improved view.

If you haven't already visited our website at www.Becoming YourBest.com, I invite you to enter your first name and e-mail address to receive a weekly e-mail, free of charge, related to each principle. The point of these e-mails is to support you and your teams as you use the blueprint. They're meant to help you establish a culture of excellence with your teams and to help these principles become habits in your personal life.

Each weekly e-mail will have a story illustrating that principle and a weekly action item that you can physically do during the week. You can adapt this to do whatever works best for you or your company. It's fun. It's exciting. It just takes desire and effort!

Business leaders love the blueprint because it is simple to implement, and yet its power and the results that it produces in their organizations are significant!

Many organizations have incorporated our blueprint and experienced tremendous results. One company that we've worked with had a 70 percent increase in revenue in just one year. The company's employees were once unhappy and disgruntled; now they are more fulfilled and doing their jobs better than ever before.

The leaders of this company cite the blueprint as the reason for their success and transformation. They have their employees get together at the beginning of each week for about five minutes to discuss a principle, and then they focus on that guiding constant throughout the week. Over time, this has had a significant influence on everyone associated with that organization—it has helped create a culture of excellence.

I've heard similar stories from many other organizations who found a way to use the blueprint with their teams and employees. Interestingly, I've also heard of people who've used this blueprint while coaching a youth sports team and I've even heard of it being used with students in a classroom. You can adapt it to whatever circumstance you're in. The point is to focus on one principle a week and over time, you and your teams can experience a significant transformation.

It is my desire that people and organizations attain principled goals. It is my desire that relationships be happy and strong, with high levels of trust. And it is my desire that all people—including you—experience the satisfaction and thrill of becoming the best they can be. Remember, your best is yet to be, and one person can make a difference!

PART ONE

Transformational Leadership

**12 Principles of
Highly Successful Leaders**

CHAPTER 1

Be True to Character

Build and be guided by a strong moral authority.

A mother once brought her child to human and civil rights pioneer Mahatma Gandhi and asked him to tell the young boy to stop eating sugar because it was not good for his diet or his developing teeth.

Gandhi replied, "I cannot tell him that. But you may bring him back in a month."

Gandhi then moved on, brushing the mother aside. She was angry; she had traveled some distance and had expected the mighty leader to support her parenting. But having little recourse, she left for her home. One month later she returned, not knowing what to expect.

The great Gandhi took the small child's hands into his own, knelt before him, and tenderly said, "Do not eat sugar, my child. It is not good for you." Then Gandhi embraced the boy and returned him to his mother.

Grateful but perplexed, the mother queried, "Why didn't you say that a month ago?"

"Well," said Gandhi, "a month ago, I was still eating sugar."

This is an example of the moral authority that comes from having a strong, principle-based character.

One of the greatest assets a person or an organization can have is strength of character based on universal principles. These behavioral laws are just as powerful as natural laws and, like them, have predictable consequences. For example, if you jump off a 40-story building, you can predict the outcome. Similarly, if you are consistently honest, you can predict that the outcome will be greater trust, opportunity, peace, and happiness, and a chance for success. On the other hand, if you lie, the result is just as predictable. You will destroy trust, lose opportunities, and perhaps end up in jail.

However, a strong character is not easily acquired. It is forged over time as we are tested and our values and judgment skills are refined and tempered. People who have a strong character withstand tests and temptations by holding true to time-honored principles that have been identified as being good and honorable throughout the course of human history.

Lead with Bedrock Principles

These bedrock principles include integrity, honesty, trustworthiness, perseverance, humility, compassion, and respect for others. When your character reflects those principles, you earn the respect and trust of those around you. Having a strong character creates a moral authority *within* you that gives you great power and credibility in your relationships, your work, and the world we share.

When you are true to your highest character, your actions reflect your beliefs and guide you through life, helping you to be your best. You feel confident, you are prepared for fresh challenges and opportunities, and you are secure in your relationships. Others are drawn to you as someone who is trustworthy and of value.

If you lack a strong character, you probably lack an internal compass for judging what is right and what is wrong, or what is good and what is bad. You also will lack confidence. You will feel out of balance and uncertain about your opportunities and your relationships. Your ability to make decisions may be severely impaired.

It is this type of strong character that provided Mahatma Gandhi and every other successful individual, parent, teacher, and leader with the moral authority required to be successful. I want to share three specific ways in which you and I can strengthen our character:

1. Be strong in the moment of choice.

2. Stand up and speak out.

3. Guard your character.

Let's look at each of these methods for strengthening and holding true to a strong character.

Be Strong in the Moment of Choice

Strength of character is demonstrated not just when things are going well, but especially when things get tough.

Character is displayed during the moment of choice (see Figure 1.1).

Imagine standing at the junction of two divergent pathways at a decisive moment in your life. One represents a decision that is in harmony with the principles and values that guide your conscience and your character. The other would conflict with those principles and values. When you make decisions based on those factors, you generally experience positive consequences and benefits.

When you don't live according to the principles and values that support your strength of character, you are usually thrown off course and out of balance. Unwanted consequences also may result. Remember that you will usually have opportunities to correct your mistakes, which beats continuing down the wrong pathway. If you choose poorly and don't correct your wrong

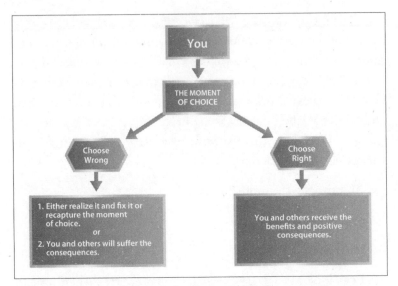

FIGURE 1.1 The Moment of Choice

decisions, your life may not follow the path you'd hoped it would follow. You make key decisions every day, and the quality of those decisions determines the quality of your life.

Truth or Consequences

A real-world example of this occurred in one of my companies when we gave our employees charge cards to purchase gasoline for company vehicles used for business purposes. One of our employees made a poor decision and displayed weakness of character by filling up her car and then handing her company charge card to a friend, who was not our employee, so that he could fuel his personal car.

Our accountants caught the suspicious double charges on the employee's credit card during a review. The gasoline station's security cameras captured all the evidence we needed. When confronted by her supervisor, the employee unwisely denied the theft. The result was that she lost her job, which was sad for everyone.

In this case, our employee actually had two moments of choice. The first came when she chose to fill up her friend's car, and the second when her supervisor asked her about the suspected theft. She had the opportunity to correct her mistake by telling her supervisor and accepting responsibility. If she had shown that she understood the error of her ways and seemed remorseful, she might have kept her job. But she did not do that, and the consequences were significant.

It is best to be strong in the initial moment of choice, but if you blow it, you will often have an opportunity to make a correction. Your objective should be to make your initial decision from a position of strength—strength of character—each and every time. Of course, while that is the ideal and the goal, we are all human. We all have moments of weakness and poor judgment, but the ability to self-correct is critical if we want to build a strong character and a life of fulfillment and meaning.

> "Character cannot be developed in ease and quiet. Only through experience of trial and suffering can the soul be strengthened, ambition inspired, and success achieved."
>
> —Helen Keller

Strength of Character Is Developed over Time

Strength of character is built over time as our principles are tested in the real world. This tempering of our character is similar to the strengthening of steel and diamonds under pressure and heat. At first, the raw materials of these substances are brittle or soft. When they have been intensely heated and compacted, however, the molecules change and the materials become some of the strongest known to man.

As your integrity, honesty, and respect for others are tested, tried, and refined, the moral fabric that makes up your character grows stronger. Over time, you become someone who can be counted on. This character establishes a moral authority *within* you that gives you great power and credibility.

Stand Up and Speak Out

Another measure of a strong character is a willingness to speak up and take a stand that you believe in, even when it is not the popular choice. Such a display of strong character is the basis of many of our most popular tales of heroism, but we can also find examples of it in our daily lives. A friend of mine was the president of a successful case lighting company in the Midwest. One of his top-level employees suffered poor judgment and made advances to a woman working in a lower-level position in the production shop. This was a violation of company policy. The two had an affair that did not end well, and the woman filed a sexual harassment lawsuit against the company.

Although a number of people in the company were aware of this activity while it was going on, no one reported it. As a result, my friend, one of the best people I know, was not aware of the problem until the lawsuit was filed. By then, it was too late. The company lost the lawsuit. The court awarded the woman $1.2 million from the company, nearly shutting down a business with more than 100 employees.

The outcome could have been far different if the top-level employee had had the strength of character to make the right decision and refrain from getting involved with another employee in the first place. In addition, the lawsuit might have been avoided if someone in the company had simply had the strength of character to come forward early on, to stand up and say something to alert the owner.

This is a real-world example of what can happen when we don't live according to guiding principles. When I heard about this, you can be sure that I reminded everyone in my businesses and organizations that we do not tolerate harassment or discrimination of any type. We made sure that every individual understood that he or she had a responsibility to report violations of our policies. We explained that a sexual harassment lawsuit could destroy a business and wipe out their jobs, and so standing up and speaking out was the right and necessary thing to do, even if it meant being "unpopular."

Character Determines Quality of Life

The actions we take, the decisions we make, and the lives we create are determined to a large degree by the content of our character.

If we fail to follow correct principles, it can have grave consequences. This isn't just a theory; I've seen it play out time and time again in the business world.

It Only Takes One Person to Stand Up and Speak Out

Following a recent keynote speech, I stayed around for lunch and listened to the next speaker, who was the former CFO of HealthSouth, which had appeared to be a very successful healthcare provider. He described how the company had slowly started to cook the books. The poor decisions began with small steps—as often happens. But soon those involved found themselves on a slippery slope. Eventually, the fraud reached the level of $3.5 billion and involved at least 17 people on the CFO's team.

The CFO's poor decisions left him living a lie that also broke up his family. He finally decided to blow the whistle by meeting with federal agents and confessing.

When the fraud became public knowledge, the company's stock dropped from $30 a share to less than $1 a share almost overnight. Investors lost billions. In his speech that day, the humbled former CFO talked about the pain that still haunts him every day. He realizes now that if only one person had taken a stand against the fraud, it might have saved countless jobs and billions of dollars.

The CFO did eventually move to correct his poor decisions by reporting the fraud to the authorities, but the consequences were still severe. He served 27 months in federal prison, as well as suffering personal humiliation and turmoil in his relationships.

To his credit, he recognized the error of his ways and worked to rebuild his character and his life. I was glad to hear that after he started making his life right again, his wife returned and remarried him. The disgraced CFO now offers himself as an example of an executive who lost his way because of a weak character. He encourages others to stand up and speak out when they see something inappropriate occurring in their own companies. One of the biggest lessons he offered was that things would have turned out vastly differently—and much better—if just one person on his team had had a strong character, taken a stand, and spoke up and said something. However, no one did that, and the results were catastrophic.

His experience provides us all with a "reality check" and invites business, community, and political leaders to make sure that they encourage those on their teams to express concerns about poor decisions, mistakes that are being made, or injustices that are being carried out. His experience should remind all of us to stand up and speak out when we see something that's not right.

A Leader with a Strong Character
Can Change the World

Perhaps one of the greatest examples of this on a global scale is the late Nelson Mandela, who opposed apartheid in his native South Africa, stood up against the powerful white-controlled government, and emerged victorious after spending 27 years in prison. Mandela's strength of character was displayed when he emerged from prison as a global hero, but made the decision to seek forgiveness, unity, and peace rather than retribution against those who had imprisoned him and suppressed the majority black population. He was not interested in a country of whites or blacks, but in a country of equals.

Mandela was elected president of South Africa, and he lived up to his pledge of unifying the historically divided nation. Shortly after taking office, he learned that the Black National Caucus had voted to eliminate the leading South African national rugby team, which had only white players and which many people saw as a reminder of apartheid.

Mandela realized that dissolving the national team would only stir resentment and anger, disrupting his efforts to unify the nation. He decided to ask the caucus to leave the team intact, even though many of his advisors opposed that decision.

Mandela spoke to the caucus members with great respect in a historic speech. He explained his vision for South Africa and asked them to stand with him. The vote was retaken, and the decision was rescinded by one vote.

Mandela's actions demonstrate the power of one person standing up and exhibiting a strong character by advocating the greater good. With the vote from the Black National Caucus in hand, Mandela enlisted the help of Francois Pienaar—the "big blonde son of apartheid"—who had long been seen by blacks as a symbol of the oppressive apartheid government. Pienaar was the star and captain of the national rugby team. When he met with Mandela, they agreed to a partnership, which reflected their strength of character. They stood up for civility and unity in South Africa, influencing millions of people around the world. After aligning with Mandela's goals, Pienaar said, "I left that first meeting with the feeling that we were in good hands in South Africa. I felt safe with him."

Two years later, the South African rugby team won the world rugby championship, a victory that united the country and symbolized a new day for its people. Despite all odds, the one who had set this in motion was Mandela, a man of remarkable character.

Have the courage to be true to character. Exercise integrity, honesty, respect, and correct principles. Whether you are the leader of a country, an organization, or a team, or simply in your daily life, be determined that you will not sit idly on the sidelines of life when issues of character come up. The strength of your character will be evident in how you conduct yourself with all people, and you will become a beacon in the world.

Guard Your Character

In Shakespeare's *Hamlet*, Polonius gives his son a "blessing" or "father's advice" as he ventures out into the world. Polonius's advice is priceless and lives across the centuries. He first advises his son to keep his thoughts to himself, to think before acting, to cherish his friends, to listen more than he talks, to seek to understand but not judge, and to neither borrow nor lend money; then, most importantly, he says:

"To thine own self be true,
And it must follow, as the night the day,
Thou canst not then be false to any man."

Being true to yourself is a hallmark of great character. In theory, this is easy to do, but it is tougher given the reality of the temptations and peer pressures encountered in daily life. In good times, it's easy to say that you will be true to your principles and values and remain strong, but your true character is formed and displayed in challenging times.

> "Be more concerned with your character than your reputation, because your character is what you really are, while your reputation is merely what others think you are."
> —John Wooden, Legendary UCLA Basketball Coach

Learn from Your Mistakes

You should never allow yourself to feel that you are a lost cause. You may have made mistakes in the past. Many people experience momentary lapses of character. It's tough to be perfect. The good news is that you can always turn your life around by deciding to be a person of integrity and honor from this point forward.

Sometimes we learn the hard way. This happened to one of our excellent summer salesmen. Based on his fabulous first summer with us, George (not his real name) was invited back to manage a team of sales reps while also working as a sales rep on the East Coast. One morning I received a call from George, who said, "I have embarrassed you, embarrassed the company, and embarrassed myself. I have to resign." Given that statement, I thought he must have been arrested or harmed someone and was calling from the police station.

"What did you do?" I asked.

George was somber as he admitted, "I lied to a customer, telling him that his neighbors had said that he should buy our products. The guy called his neighbors and confirmed that my story was not true. I am so sorry. Now you can see why I have to resign."

I told George that I appreciated his call. Then, I told him that sometimes the best way to *really* learn to live a principle is by feeling the painful consequences when you have violated it. More important, I told him: "I would like you to go back out, apologize to the customer one more time, tell him that you were wrong, and tell him that you are committed to never doing this again. Then determine in your own heart that you will live honestly to a T."

George agreed to do exactly that. He worked for another eight years as an outstanding contributor to our organization and went on to become the CEO of a very successful firm that has a reputation not only for industry leadership, but also for unquestioned business integrity.

Leading with Character: An Assessment

My response to George's call and our treatment of him reflect the principles and values that make up the character of our company. We hold an annual retreat for organizational and planning purposes, but we also use this occasion to review the company's operating values and principles—in other words, the company's character. We have done this for more than 25 years. Included in our assessment are these values:

- We treat people right.

- We don't lie, cheat, or steal, nor do we tolerate any among us who do. (This is adapted from the Honor Code of the U.S. Air Force Academy.)

We also distribute a list of questions on ethics to help us evaluate our decisions based upon integrity, honesty, and respect for others:

1. Is it legal? Will I be violating either civil law or company policy?

2. Is it balanced? Is it fair to all concerned in both the short term and the long term? Does it promote healthy relationships?

3. How will it make me feel about myself?

4. Will it make me feel proud?

5. Would I feel good if my decision were published in the newspaper?

6. Would I feel good if my family knew about my decision?

You've heard the old adage, "Cheaters never prosper." We are more effective when we steer our employees to the high ground and then give them as much support as we can to help them stay there. We do this by clearly defining what we are all about. The successful international businessman Jon Huntsman, Sr., explained it well when he said: "Winners never cheat and cheaters never win."

There is always a price to pay for dishonesty, whether you are caught or not. It is a corrupting force, and eventually liars are buried by their own falsehoods. Those who act without integrity, honesty, and respect for others will be caught and punished, either by the law or by the power of natural consequences.

This is true not only for individuals, but for organizations as well. Those businesses that serve their customers and put them first tend to thrive and endure, while those that see their customers as prey will eventually cut their own throats or rot from within. We believe that great businesses are those that hire people of good character and then support and encourage them. It's the inside-out method put into practice at the organizational level. If you staff a company with talented men and women of good character, your business will reflect their principles and values.

What Could Challenge You and Test Your Character?

As you move through life, you'll probably need to remind yourself often of these words: *to thine own self be true*. And you're just as likely to have daily opportunities to answer the critical question in your moment of choice: *Will I be true to the principles of character?*

When the waters are calm, it's easier to respond, "I will!" But what about those times when things heat up and you're under blistering stress? Those moments put your character to the test.

> "Good character is not formed in a week or a month. It is created little by little, day by day. Protracted and patient effort is needed to develop good character. A man's character is his guardian divinity."
>
> —Heraclitus

My wife and I are proud of all six of our children because each of them has displayed strong moral character as he or she has reached adulthood. They've often exceeded our expectations and our dreams in both their accomplishments and their strength of character. When our son Steven was in the middle of weapons school training—the U.S. Air Force's Top Gun program—he made a serious error during a night run on a bombing range in simulated combat.

He dropped a bomb in the wrong place—on the wrong bombing range during a live simulation. No one was injured, fortunately, but my son was horrified. Because of the nature of these exercises, however, no one knew of Steven's mistake.

This was the ultimate moment of choice: Would he do the right thing and preserve his character, or would he cover up what nobody else would ever really know about, but violate his character standards?

Upon landing, he went to his commanding officer and reported his error, even though he knew it might have prevented him from being selected as a Top Gun pilot.

Even if he hadn't been selected, I would still have been proud of my son, and I would have encouraged him to be proud of himself because he had showed great strength of character by being honest and trustworthy. Apparently his commander felt the same way. Steve was selected as a Top Gun pilot and graduated near the top of his class, receiving a prestigious award upon graduation. He went on to become a Top Gun instructor.

Three Keys to Open Your Life to Success and Fulfillment

This chapter has provided you with three powerful keys to having a strong character.

1. Be strong in the moment of choice.

2. Stand up and speak out.

3. Guard your character.

These three qualities are literally pillars of strength in your life, your relationships, and your organization. There are many rewards for building your life based on proven values and the highest principles. Some of them come with medals and public honors, but I believe the greatest are those that are nurtured within us. I'm proud that my son belongs to the Top Gun elite, but I'm prouder still of what lies within his heart and the content of his character. I want you to feel that way about yourself and your organization—strong, confident, and ready for any challenge based upon a foundation that nothing could shake.

Leadership Action Steps

1. Begin using the Becoming Your Best blueprint. Visit our website at www.BecomingYourBest.com and enter your first name and e-mail.

2. Ponder and write your response to questions such as these: Why is character so important in my life? What principles determine my character? What compass do I live by? Do my actions reflect my or our core values based upon correct principles?

3. When you're faced with a moment of choice, do the right thing, the best thing!

4. Resolve that you will never lie, cheat, or steal. Remember, if you aren't telling the whole truth, you aren't telling the truth.

5. Guard and protect your character, your honor, your integrity, and your name.

6. Stand up and speak out when you see something that isn't right.

7. Keep your word. Do what you say you will do. Be dependable.

8. If you're not sure whether something is ethical, err on the conservative side.

9. Be accurate in your descriptions. Underpromise and overdeliver.

10. Do not talk negatively about others in their absence. On the contrary, find something good to say about them.

11. If you're not sure about a decision, ask yourself: *Will it make me proud? Would I feel good if this were published in the newspaper? What if my family knew about it?*

12. Remember and live this principle: "To thine own self be true and thou canst not then be false to any man."

CHAPTER 2

Lead with a Vision

Put your vision to work and get
outstanding results.

I attended an international conference of business executives in
Istanbul, Turkey, that featured as guest speakers the president
of Coca-Cola and the president of Mercedes-Benz. In separate
speeches, both of these high-level business leaders said that they
don't believe in mission statements.

I was intrigued by their comments. They described how
important it was to them, as individuals and as company presidents, to have clear, inspiring, and transformational visions of
who they were and where they wanted to go. I believe that what
they were saying was that we need to be careful not to create a
"mission statement," hang it on the wall, and feel that this makes
us good to go from there on out. Indeed, that does miss the point.

Both men described their visions for their companies. They
talked about making the world a better place through excellence.
Each believed that he was qualified to achieve his vision because
of his unique skills, resources, assets, and abilities. Their visions
not only propelled them to where they are today, but also will
determine their direction into the future.

In nearly all individuals, classrooms, teams, divisions, or organizations where we see sustained excellence, there is an inspiring and well-articulated vision.

Regardless of whether they call it a dream, a mission statement, or a cause, most highly successful leaders have a vision that helps to inspire and drive them.

President Reagan once said, "To grasp and hold a vision, that is the very essence of successful leadership." An inspiring and well-articulated vision can transform your life, an organization, and even the world.

What's important is to actually have a clear vision! Many people have written and talked about the importance of a vision, but I've been in many organizations that are still struggling with the idea of an inspiring vision, how to create one, and how to lead with a vision. In a highly complex and competitive world, the need to have a clear and compelling vision—both for an individual and for an organization—has never been greater.

While it is deeply personal, a vision will eventually touch others. It generally germinates deep within you, and you can feel its power as it grows from its beginning as a mere thought to its transformation into a physical creation and reality; something magical seems to blossom when we lead with a vision.

> "A rock pile ceases to be a rock pile the
> moment a single man contemplates it, bearing
> within him the image of a cathedral."
> —Antoine De Saint-Exupery

This growth happens naturally as you ponder your own unique vision, purpose, gifts, and abilities and as you realize how these things can be wonderfully manifested in your life and in the lives of others. The same process occurs within an organization, which should be guided by a vision that defines its unique purpose.

In reality, every person is connected to at least one organization in some way. An organization may be a couple, a family, a community, a team, a business, a church, a service group, a country, or a world, to name just a few examples. The best leadership often occurs when you connect your personal uniqueness to that of your organization(s).

Leadership might be aptly described as a type of stewardship. Like every other person, you have a unique set of talents and skills. The real question is how you will use those talents, circumstances, abilities, and skills to bless others—and, in the process, to realize increased happiness, peace, and fulfillment in your own life. You are a more effective leader when you think in terms of being a responsible and an effective steward, guided by a vision.

Your personal or organizational vision is designed to best use your talents to live more fully, enjoy greater abundance, and better contribute to your organization and to the world. It is impossible to do good without having a positive impact on others and even the world around you. The fact is, you make a difference, one way or another, and you should never underestimate the power of your influence.

A vision aims for a high level of achievement. It is not the same as goals or objectives, which are created after your vision is formed. We will discuss setting goals in the next chapter, which focuses on managing with a plan. A vision is a high-level desired outcome or accomplishment that you hope to achieve. A vision is how you describe yourself, your team, or your organization from the 35,000-foot view.

Throughout this chapter, we'll look at three powerful aspects of an inspiring, guiding vision for any area of your life, whether it's related to you personally, your organization, or your teams and relationships. The three areas that I wish to address are:

1. Attributes of a transformational vision

2. Create and evaluate your own personal and organizational vision

3. Transformational results that flow from a principle-based, inspiring vision

Attributes of a Transformational Vision

A vision can be transformational. When you have a clear, compelling vision, you transform the effort, the conversation, and the results of not only your own life, but the life of your organization—whether that organization is a company, a community, a team, or a family.

One of the most inspiring examples of a simple yet powerful vision was the declaration by President Kennedy in 1962 that the United States would send a man to the moon and return him safely before the end of the decade. This vision focused an entire nation and directed it toward an inspirational cause. As a result of realizing that vision and that goal, our country and the world have never been the same. We were all changed for the better.

I have studied and observed outstanding individuals and organizations domestically and internationally, and I've found that they definitely have one thing in common: an inspiring and deeply felt vision that guides them toward their best. I have also observed that there are a number of key attributes that are typically present in most individual or organizational visions and make those visions very effective. Some of these attributes apply to an individual vision, some apply to an organizational vision, and some apply to both. Let's look at a few of these attributes.

1. A vision sets a positive and meaningful direction with a purpose and a cause. It rallies support that results in commitments and new levels of contribution.

2. A vision carries a sense of urgency and mission. When a vision is based on principles, this sense of urgency encompasses more than revenue and return on investment. The ultimate virtue of the cause invites unusual effort and commitment.

3. A good vision is inspiring. It can make your efforts noble and meaningful. You are inspired to fully give your best in cooperation with your colleagues, and together you achieve your best.

4. A vision is clear, simple, and easy to remember. If it's long and wordy, it tends to be difficult for people to remember.

5. A vision provides the desired direction, purpose, and inspiration in the absence of supervision. When employees with an effective vision are left to their own decision making and devices, they will have a clear sense of direction and be empowered by the vision.

6. A vision encourages the alignment of people and effort around the vision. Your team members feel encouraged and empowered by it. They willingly subscribe to it and join their commitment to your conviction as the leader.

7. A vision represents the heart and soul of an individual or the group. It embodies the values and personal needs for contributing to something bigger. The vision generates passion and energy.

8. A vision is developed through individual and shared leadership. Each participant in the vision is a "leader" who contributes uniqueness to the whole.

9. A vision is long term and should be modified with care. The vision unifies individuals by giving them a common purpose. It does not change quickly. President Kennedy's vision was accomplished after a massive nine-year effort to put a man on the moon.

10. A vision is clearly communicated to all members of the team or the community through centers of influence. The vision is lived, modeled, and taught over and over again by key stakeholders and to one another.

11. A vision becomes anchored in the individual or organizational culture. It becomes part of the conscience of each person it touches. A test of the organizational vision is how well each person understands it, is influenced by it, and can explain it.

I have seen some visions that can be stated in just a few words and some that require several paragraphs (which is all right for a corporate vision if everyone can still understand and internalize it). The vision works best when expressed in a way that strikes a strong emotional chord for you and your organization. The value of the vision is what it communicates to you and to others. If it is clear and describes the desired direction of leadership, then it ensures that you're headed in the right direction.

When our son Rob was a fighter pilot and an inspector, he would often visit squadrons and see that their leaders had posted written vision or mission statements on the walls. He would grab pilots and ask them what the vision was in their squadron, and nine times out of ten, they didn't know—even though it was written on the walls around them.

I've done the same thing in the business world and received a similar response. When the employees don't know what the vision is, this thwarts the whole purpose of having it in the first place. If the vision just sits on the wall, then it's not a vision, it's a wall ornament!

A significant and effective vision or mission statement, whatever you want to call it, shouldn't be a wall ornament. If it is personal, it should reflect the driving purpose in your life. If it is a vision for your business, it should reflect the driving purpose of the business, while also providing clear direction for all executives and employees.

If the vision is effective, it will burn deeply within your heart and mind. If we're talking about an organizational vision, the employees will understand it, and it will give them a clear sense of direction and guidance, even without a leader being present.

> "Cherish your visions and your dreams,
> as they are the children of your soul, the
> blueprints of your ultimate achievements."
> —Napoleon Hill

An inspiring and effective vision will become your guide for who you are and who you want to become and will ultimately determine the culture and direction in your organization.

Create and Evaluate Your Own Personal and Organizational Vision

We've reviewed some of the attributes of an effective vision. Now, let's get specific and touch on a few important points to remember as you write or refine your personal or organizational vision.

I suggest that you start at the personal level, then apply this powerful practice to the organizations in your life. As we go through this activity together and develop a vision, you can use your journal or notebook as a place to capture the impressions you get from each question.

Every time we do this exercise and develop a vision in our seminars, our participants say that it has a significant impact on them. It gives leaders and employees a chance to step back and reflect on what's most important to them. The first few questions listed here are simply designed to get your creative juices flowing and get your mind focused on what's most important to you, before you write your actual vision. As you go through these questions, please take your time and put some thought into it. This isn't something that you want to rush through and finish quickly. Answer the following questions:

- What do you really want to achieve in life, or what contributions do you want to make to others, your organization, your community, and the world?

- What are the unique skills, talents, and abilities that you can build upon for the benefit of others? List your unique skills or talents.

- How do you hope others will describe you when you are nearing the end of your life? How do you hope others will describe your organization?

- If you had unlimited time and resources and could do whatever you want, what would that be?

- As you contemplate what you (or your organization) are capable of accomplishing, what idea or thought takes your breath away?

These questions are meant to help you get started and to help you think about what's most important in your life. They can help you identify and describe what is best about you.

After reflecting on your answers, you should be ready to write your vision. Sometimes people have a hard time knowing where to start; just put pen to paper and write whatever comes to mind. The art is in the start!

You can state your vision in a couple of sentences, or it can take a few paragraphs, depending on what works best for you. In addition, I suggest using "I am" statements whenever possible. In other words, don't hope or try; describe yourself or your organization in the present tense, as if you were already there. Create the mental reality before you create the physical reality.

For example, you might say, "I am a person of deep character and integrity." Or you might say, "I am kind and caring, and I treat people the way I hope they would treat me." You could also say about your organization, "We are the number one provider of _____ products in the world!" Those are just three quick examples.

Let's begin; go ahead and write your vision. Let the ideas flow and see what comes from deep within you. The result is your vision!

> On a device or a piece of paper,
> write your personal vision now.

How was that experience of writing your vision? Usually, it's a refreshing and liberating feeling to see the words written or typed. It's one thing to think about your vision, but it's much more powerful to see it in written words.

While you may improve the format by making some refinements over time, don't forget the substance of your vision. You can polish it as you respond to your feelings and impressions, but you should modify it only with care. Allow this vision to create a direction for your life or your organization, and allow it to affect everything that you do.

To better help you find a way to describe your vision, I've provided a few examples of effective personal and organizational vision statements. Remember the alternative words that describe a vision, such as *mission*, *inspiration*, or *purpose*.

Just as when you climb from peak to peak, you gain whole new scenic views, when you identify an inspiring vision, your initial vision helps you climb to see an expanded vision or a new set of possibilities. Frequently one vision inspires another. Let's look at some examples of personal visions and then move to some organizational visions.

Examples of Personal Vision

- I am an individual of unquenchable curiosity and feverishly inventive imagination.

- I shall not fear anyone, only God. I shall not bear ill will toward anyone. I shall conquer untruth with truth. And, in resisting untruth, I shall put up with all suffering.

- I shall live this day as if it were my last!

- I achieve the seemingly impossible.

- I am the master of my fate and the captain of my soul.

- I am a person of total integrity.

- I am physically fit and take care of myself. I work to maximize my health, energy, and peace of mind.

- I am a game changer! I am making a difference for good personally, in my relationships, and within my organization.

- I am leaving the world a better place than I found it.

- I consistently ask myself what my best or my organization's best looks like, and I work doggedly to get to the best that can be.

- I am not complacent. I am vigilant and keep looking for ways to improve.

- I am a faithful and loyal spouse and enjoy a deep relationship with my family.

As you can see in these examples, a vision doesn't have to be long and wordy. Sometimes there is great power in being short and concise; other times your vision might need several paragraphs. Again, the power is in actually having a vision that's written and clearly understood.

Organizational Vision Examples

Here are some examples of an organizational vision from various industry leaders. Each of these organizations has made a significant impact on the world. As you read these organizational examples, consider your own organization. The real test is to ask yourself whether your organization's vision statement describes the organization's purpose and influences the desired behavior in the absence of supervision. Does the vision statement keep the organization focused on what matters most?

Let's get on with some examples. You can probably guess who some of these organizations are!

- To bring the best personal computing experience around the world through innovative hardware, software, and Internet offerings.

- To be the company that best understands and satisfies the product, service, and self-fulfillment needs of women—globally.

- People working together as one global company for aerospace leadership.

- We—employees, customers, and community partners—together form a force for positive local and global change, dedicated to bettering standards of living and the environment where we and our customers live and work.

- To make the world better through transparency of information and increased sharing of thoughts and ideas.

- To develop a perfect search engine.

- Create experiences that combine the magic of software with the power of Internet services across a world of devices.

- To carry on his legacy of innovative thinking, whether to develop products that help athletes of every level of ability reach their potential, or to create business opportunities that set us apart from the competition and provide value for our shareholders.

- We are Ladies and Gentlemen serving Ladies and Gentlemen.

- Double revenue over the next 10 years.

- To help supply all the people of the earth with clean water within the next 10 years.

- We do not lie, steal, or cheat, nor tolerate among us anyone who does.

- Dedication to the highest quality of customer service delivered with a sense of warmth, friendliness, individual pride, and company spirit.

- Help people to save money so that they can live better.

- With malice toward none, with charity for all, with firmness in the right as God gives us to see the right.

Whether you want to articulate, refine, or revise a personal, relationship, or organizational vision, you need only a sheet of paper. Let the words of the vision flow from the very center of your heart and mind. Soon, you will know that it represents what you are all about and that it represents the highest and best that you can do.

Recently, after a seminar with a world-class shipbuilding company, the CEO said to me at the end of the day, "My take-home from this experience today is to go back and reflect upon our vision. How does it look today? Am I communicating this vision to all who are associated with our great cause and company?" This is a wonderful example of what highly successful leaders continually do.

Transformational Results that Flow from a Principle-Based, Inspiring Vision

Once an inspired vision has been written and understood, it provides direction and clarity that leads to achieving your best results.

I've seen the powerful and positive impact of a vision in nearly every field I've researched. I've witnessed the impact that a new leader with a strong vision can have on a troubled team or a failing organization. I have seen this repeatedly in the lives of top producers and also in the lives of successful parents.

These individuals and organizations know what they are about, and their vision is clear. The vision is regularly discussed and understood by everyone working together.

Now that we've looked at personal and organizational visions and seen some examples, let me share with you some personal experiences that illustrate the transformative power of a vision.

Southwest Airlines: Mile-High Vision

I witnessed the stunning influence of an organizational vision that is now deeply embedded in the culture of the business when I was on a recent Southwest Airlines flight. Anyone who's flown on Southwest knows that it has a clear vision that is often on display and apparent in its employees, both on the ground and in the air. Its vision, last time I checked, was:

> "Dedication to the highest quality of
> Customer Service delivered with a
> sense of warmth, friendliness, individual
> pride, and company spirit."

While boarding a Southwest flight, I noticed that the crew seemed understaffed. There wasn't even a pilot in the cockpit! Everyone was running around frantically trying to get the bags on the plane for an on-time departure. When I looked out the window from my seat, I saw something amazing: the captain of the flight was down helping to load bags!

I could see that he was pitching in and was engaged with the baggage crew and the flight attendants, all of whom manifested Southwest's uplifting spirit of service and camaraderie.

That's just one of many examples of how Southwest has embodied its vision. Remember, a vision is vital to the success of a team—a clear, united vision can help you break through barriers that hold you back so that you can truly become your best. In this case, the employees of Southwest were guided by a clear and compelling vision that is deeply embedded in the company culture.

Here is another example that illustrates the power of a personal vision.

"I Will Be Your Top Salesman"

My company was holding its annual event for college students who were employed by our publishing company as sales representatives. Each would soon be assigned an area somewhere in the country to represent our firm in selling children's books and other educational products.

During this week of "sales school," we taught these energetic college students ethics, organization, sales skills, and product knowledge, and we provided them with examples of persistence. As part of the training, we also explained the many weekly incentives that we had and talked about the big Hawaii trip that we used to reward our top producers. Everyone who hit a certain level of sales would qualify, and the competition to be among the top sales representatives was intense.

This was a time of excitement and great energy. Hundreds of these students would work 75 hours a week during the summer and earn enough to pay for the upcoming academic year at their university.

Well-recognized motivational speakers were part of the week's program; they included respected leaders like Denis Waitley, Zig Ziglar, Norman Vincent Peale, Stephen R. Covey, Earl Nightingale, Ira Hayes, Charlie "Tremendous" Jones, and Doug Snarr, to name a few. Needless to say, this was a great time as these individuals assessed their potential and what they could accomplish during the summer. In a sense, this experience set them on a "success pathway" for their careers.

At the end of the third of five days of training, there was a knock on my hotel room door. I answered and saw a skinny, sickly looking kid who was about six feet tall. He introduced himself to me as John. He then said, "I just wanted to introduce myself and let you know that I will be your number one salesman this summer." I thought to myself, "Yeah, right!" Despite my disbelief, I gave him encouragement, adding that I would like to stay in touch with him as he gave his very best throughout the summer. He said, "Okay, but don't forget: I will be your number one salesman."

John had an inspiring, burning personal vision. It was a huge idea that had entered his heart and mind from deep within and that subsequently provided his capacity for leadership and action.

> "I skate to where the puck is going
> to be, not where it has been."
> —Wayne Gretzky

He actually started off a little slowly, but by the fourth and fifth weeks of the summer, he was among our top sales representatives. By the tenth week, he was consistently one of our best, and by the end of the summer, he finished at the top. That's right— John was the number one sales representative in the company.

Year after year, I observed that our top-performing sales representatives had a vision of what they wanted to accomplish; it was this vision that drove them on when others faltered along the way. I saw in them a deep personal vision that provided the source for successful leadership and stewardship. I understood what they were experiencing because I had felt exactly the same way, and my vision had driven me on!

Standards of Business: ExxonMobil

Another example of the impact of vision on behavior and world-class leadership was illustrated by an experience shared in a 2013 speech by Rex W. Tillerson, the chairman and CEO of ExxonMobil.

In the speech, which was featured in the Brigham Young University alumni magazine, Rex discussed his company's vision, which is built upon integrity and guiding principles of leadership. ExxonMobil refers to this vision as its Standards of Business. This vision essentially states: "Every employee is personally responsible for the safety of themselves, the public, and others at ExxonMobil; each must comply with all the laws and regulations; and everyone is expected to be honest and ethical at all times." It goes on to state an even higher standard, "Even where the law is permissive, the corporation chooses the course of highest integrity." This way of doing business is a powerful and inspiring vision that provides direction in the absence of supervision.

Tillerson shared an experience that had occurred many years before he became CEO of his company, saying that it inspired the implementation of this vision. "I was sent to Yemen, on the heels of a civil war, because the government was aggregating our contract and a competitor had bribed the president. I was sent in to either sort it out or turn it over to the international arbitration court. The very first meeting I had with the Yemenite administrator was late at night at his house. We talked a little bit, and he said, 'Well, Mr. Tillerson, I look forward to working with you. The only thing I need you to do is to wire $20 million to this bank account.'"

Tillerson said that he was stunned by the bold statement, which was made in 1995. He was just 43 years old. "This was the first time I had been overseas by myself to do a deal like this. I paused a minute, looked at him, and said, 'Excellency, I can't do that. If that's the basis on which you want to do business, then we can't do any business. I appreciate your receiving me at your home.' And then I left."

Tillerson said that on the flight home, he thought: "Golly, I just walked away from a $4.5 billion deal." He'd done it without consulting his bosses, and he wondered how they would respond.

"When I got to Dallas and told my boss what had happened, he said, without hesitation, 'Fine. We're outta there.'"

Three weeks later, a letter arrived from the same person who'd suggested the payment. He wanted to know when Tillerson was returning. After consulting with his superiors, Tillerson flew back to meet with him, curious as to how this meeting would go, since he had refused to pay up.

The bribe was never again mentioned. The future CEO said that he then realized: "All I had to do was say no in a respectful way."

Often, it's as simple as that: be respectful and say, "No, I'm sorry, we don't do that. If those are the rules, my company and I can't work here." I've had to do that a couple of times in my business career, and it has worked out the same way. As soon as someone figured out that no meant no, he stopped asking.

Because of a clear, inspiring, principle-based vision, Rex Tillerson didn't have to look right or left, or even second-guess himself. He was able to firmly lead with a vision.

The Power of a Vision

I'd like to reiterate the three things I outlined on leading with a vision.

First, I described the components of a transformational vision. A vision is transformational when it inspires us with passion. Visions are effective when they are clear and well communicated. They will provide direction and purpose, and give you and your team a clear destination.

I outlined some tips and ideas on ways for an individual or an organization to create a vision.

I also illustrated why visions are vital to the success of organizations. The vision should be reinforced often: during meetings, in newsletters, and at corporate gatherings. A vision statement should not become a wall ornament. It should be adopted and embraced by the culture of the organization or business so that it guides all team members, especially when there is no supervisor available.

That's the power of a vision! The vision of one can influence many. Remember, your vision springs from deep within you as you reflect on your own uniqueness and how you can contribute to a better organization and a better world. When you create and live with a vision, you are actually creating your future. The mental creation precedes the physical creation of reality. As another famous politician, Sir Winston Churchill, once noted: "The empires of the future are the empires of the mind."

Once a person or organization has a clear vision, that person or organization is well positioned to set clear and measurable goals to accomplish that vision. Without a vision, the goals are less likely to be centered on a specific desired outcome. It's the vision that creates the direction and atmosphere to develop goals and a plan to get there.

Frequently our best vision is discovered through hardship and adversity. It is through these experiences that we find out who we are and develop a greater capacity to give to others. When you do good things for others, you influence your organization, your community, and the world in a positive way. You can make a difference by living with a vision.

Every age needs men and women who create and live with visions for new and better days. Through ups and downs, through challenges and victories, while facing threats and embracing opportunities, you can follow a clear and inspiring vision. It will help you achieve breathtaking success that opens new opportunities. An inspired and principle-based vision will have an enormous positive impact on you, on your organization, and on the world.

Leadership Action Steps

1. Remember that the vision of one can influence many.

2. The vision springs from deep within you as you reflect on your own uniqueness and how you can contribute to a better organization and a better world.

3. The mental creation precedes the physical creation and the future reality.

4. Consider leadership as a type of stewardship. What can you do with the opportunity, position, gifts, talents, and skills that you have to contribute?

5. A clear organizational vision isn't a wall ornament! It provides leadership in the absence of supervision and creates a purpose.

6. Frequently, your best vision is discovered through hardship and adversity. Through these experiences, you discover who you really are and develop a great capacity to give to others.

7. You can create a personal vision, a corporate vision, and a vision for your family.

8. When writing your personal vision, use "I am" statements as if you were already there, rather than the word *try* or *hope*. For example, "I am a person of deep character and integrity!"

CHAPTER 3

Manage with a Plan

Set goals and take the right steps to achieve big results.

Angela Wolf was blinded at the age of 12 when a doctor gave her an overdose of vitamin A. This led to a rare condition that produced excess brain fluid, and the resulting pressure destroyed her optic nerves. The young girl responded to her tragic loss of eyesight by relying on her incredible inner vision. She dreamed of what she wanted to do to create that vision, then she developed a specific, step-by-step plan for her life, one that refused to accept any limitations.

Despite her disability, Angela set an ambitious goal: to become a teacher. She underwent training for the blind to learn how to adapt and overcome the challenges that those without sight faced. She then attended a normal high school in Louisiana and earned a humanities degree at the University of Texas. But Angela did not stop there. She went on to obtain a master's degree in education and received her teaching certificate in 2005.

Her scholastic achievements are only part of Angela's list of accomplishments. During her college years, she became an activist for the blind and president of the National Association of Blind Students. She made a mark along with making her grades.

Angela followed her inner vision and managed her plan with a deep commitment that brought her great success. She soared above limitations, exceeded expectations, and always worked to be her best. The outstanding efforts of this Austin, Texas, elementary school teacher were recognized in 2011 when the National Federation of the Blind named her Blind Educator of the Year.

With a Plan, You Can!

The secret to getting things done in any area of your life is to use your imagination to create a vision, then develop goals as part of a long-range plan that supports the vision. Finally, of course, you have to summon the energy and determination to carry out that plan, just as Angela did!

"I recall thinking almost from the beginning that regardless of my blindness, I could do whatever I wanted to do in life," she said in an interview. "Whatever I want to do, whether it's finding my way through a building or learning to be a teacher, I just have to figure out the 'how.' I have to do things a bit differently, but, in the end, I get it done."

As Angela's story demonstrates, one of the greatest skills you can master on your way to becoming your best is the ability to develop a thoughtful plan that allows you to manage your work and your life. Having a plan prepares you to take control of your life, to handle challenges, and to reach your full potential. It also helps you create order amid chaos, so that you can find solutions where others see only challenges.

This guiding constant focuses on the things you can do to manage your career and your life effectively by having a plan. Almost anyone can do it, but it takes discipline and effort. Angela wrote her own life story by creating a vision and then coming up with a plan consisting of small steps that led to big accomplishments.

Once she had mastered the small steps of dealing with her blindness by learning to read Braille and move about with a cane, Angela moved on to earning her college degree and her teaching certificates.

An important element of creating a plan for your career or your business is enlisting allies along the way who can support you. These may be your coworkers, your bosses, your suppliers or service providers, or even your customers and clients. As a teacher with a serious disability, Angela makes her students her allies in the classroom (see Figure 3.1).

Imagine trying to control, let alone teach, a roomful of very active children without being able to see them. Angela overcomes that problem by winning the hearts and minds of her students, so that they want to help her succeed and achieve their shared goals in the classroom.

Every leader can learn from Angela Wolf. She developed an inner vision and a specific plan. She then began by mastering

FIGURE 3.1 Angela in her classroom.

small steps that led to greater achievements. When she was faced with challenges, she found solutions and implemented them by adjusting her plan, troubleshooting, recalibrating, and taking action.

No Title Necessary

While her job title is "teacher," Angela is a highly successful leader when it comes to managing her own life, personally as well as professionally. She began with a vision and created a plan to succeed as a person first, and then as a teacher and a member of her community.

Creating a plan to be a loving parent and spouse or a great member of your community may not win you accolades in the media or national awards, but it is still a very valuable and laudable mission in life. Whether your plan is to change your life or to change the world, the first step is to define what the best looks like for you. You don't need the title of *manager* to develop a vision and a plan; anyone and everyone can do this!

> "Quality is never an accident; it is always the result of high intention, sincere effort, intelligent direction and skillful execution; it represents the wise choice of many alternatives."
>
> —William Foster

If you actually have the title of corporate manager or a similar work role, there is a subtle, yet powerful lesson to be learned from Angela Wolf. She had to define what her best looked like. In the same way, those who manage organizations and businesses must establish what the best looks like for their team, division, or company. But there is a critical difference that managers have to face in their planning. They are most effective at realizing their goals when they set up systems and structures to ensure that the people around them adopt the vision and work toward achieving the best outcomes and performances. This is what Angela did in the classroom, and it is what you can do, too.

Regardless of your title, there are three powerful things that you and I can do as individuals or in organizations that are game changers in every aspect of life. They are:

1. Set annual goals and develop a plan to achieve them.

2. Plan for the unexpected.

3. Manage for results.

Let's look at each of these in greater detail.

Set Annual Goals and Develop a Plan to Achieve Them

In the course of spending years researching this topic, I've found that less than 10 percent of people have specific, written goals. Yet, many studies indicate that when goals are specific and written, the likelihood of them being achieved increases significantly. In fact, our research indicates that people are nearly 90 percent more likely to achieve a goal if it's *clearly written* and *referred to often*. In talking to participants in our seminars and others around the world, we've learned that this process of developing annual goals and a plan has changed many lives for the better and helped make employees much more productive and efficient. I've found that many businesses we've worked with had at least some basic goals, but in working with their leaders, we refined those goals and their objectives. Once we did that, their effectiveness increased and they achieved significantly higher levels of success. In addition to the business aspect, I've heard of parents repairing their relationships with their children, CEOs getting balance back in their lives, people losing weight and restoring their health, and many other individual success stories when people start using goals effectively.

I often ask our seminar participants and other clients about their experiences in setting and achieving goals. As I mentioned, they report a wide variety of experiences. The most successful individuals always seem to be the most aggressive in developing plans for their endeavors. Those who have had less success often report that they haven't developed formal plans or that they abandoned those plans at some point. The most frequent feedback I receive on this topic sounds like this: "I haven't had a lot of experience with goals, and I was really never taught what works and how to use goals effectively." It's really not important where you've been or what you've done in the past; the question is, what will you do in the future?

This relatively simple and repeatable process allows you to become more proactive and engaged because you are taking responsibility for your own growth and success.

Let me introduce a very effective way to set individual goals; it's called *Roles and Goals*. Using Roles and Goals can help you or your team take the impossible and make it possible. This method of goal setting is extremely effective. It will bring balance to your life or to the lives of your employees. It will help reduce stress and increase flexibility. It helps you schedule your priorities, rather than being a victim of your schedule!

You can use Roles and Goals to set clear and actionable goals and then develop a plan to make those goals a reality. This isn't about creating goals just to check off something that's on a list. You set fulfilling goals so that you can enjoy the journey as you carry out your plan. If your overall vision is to strengthen your relationship with your spouse, then you might set the goal of having two enjoyable dates a month without the children. In this example, you aren't just checking it off; you are purposely finding a way to make your life richer and your marriage more rewarding.

Now and then I run into an accomplished person who has never developed a formal process for setting goals and pursuing them. My friend Brian surprised me when he said that he's never had a written goal. This surprised me because he has a master's degree and works as a successful CPA. I always viewed him as a top-notch, successful guy, so I wondered just how much more he could accomplish if he set goals and then developed a plan to accomplish them.

What caught my attention was that although he appeared to be very successful, Brian told me that he felt empty inside. He reluctantly admitted that he felt that he could accomplish so much more in his life and in his family. Brian felt that there was something missing.

After we discussed the power of Roles and Goals and explained the steps, he decided to give it a try and start small. He came up with five written goals.

One of his goals was to run a 5K race in less than 30 minutes by July 30th, which initially seemed like an impossible goal for Brian. He never would have attempted to run such a race if he hadn't written it down as a goal and then followed a step-by-step plan to prepare himself for it. He accomplished all of his original five goals by the end of the year. Thanks to this simple, yet very effective tool of goal setting, he's doing amazing things that he had never thought possible and building wonderful memories in the process. Brian is now a firm believer, and last year he added many more goals to his list.

There are many methods and techniques for setting goals. My team and I have put years of effort and research into finding a way to help people change their lives for the better by setting and accomplishing goals. We wanted to have a process that anyone can follow, one that has a powerful impact and brings balance to people's lives. The response from almost everyone who has used Roles and Goals has been overwhelmingly positive and life changing. As you read through the steps I've listed here, imagine the effect this process would have if everyone in your organization—from the CEO to line employees—used it.

Let's go over the ABCs for using Roles and Goals.

1. **Review your vision and the key roles in your life.** Whether you are doing this as an individual, a couple, or a team or within an organization, you begin by aligning your goals with your vision. That's why we always start with the vision.

   Next, you divide your life into key roles. These roles might include parent, friend, manager, employee, professional, student, citizen, or church member. You also have the "personal" role—in other words, maintaining your physical, mental, emotional, and spiritual health. My dear friend Stephen Covey would call this personal role "sharpening the saw." When you divide your life into your various roles, this creates an opportunity for a balanced approach. It helps prevent misalignment of priorities and helps you focus your time on what matters most.

2. **Develop annual goals in each role using the SMART method.** Research has shown that the more specific and measurable a goal is, the more likely it is to be achieved. The SMART method, based on an acronym, is a great way to create high-quality goals and then assess your progress toward achieving them. SMART refers to setting goals that are:

   Specific
   Measurable
   Achievable
   Relevant
   Time-specific

   One of the most common mistakes I see in goals is that they aren't specific or measurable enough. The more specific and measurable the goal, the more likely it is to be achieved. During corporate training, we help leaders and teams develop actionable plans and goals using the SMART framework. Oftentimes, this will have a significant impact on their ability to successfully develop and execute their plan.

Once you've reviewed your vision, determined your roles, and set SMART goals within each role, you're ready for the next step.

3. **Share your goals.** Send your goals to a few friends, mentors, advisors, or others who you admire and respect who can give feedback that is worth following. For example, each year at the end of December, I'll send several people an account of my goals for the year and how well I did in achieving them, in my view. Then I'll send them my goals for the new year. This makes my goals official and makes me accountable. According to one study, you're 33 percent more likely to achieve your goals if you're accountable to someone.

I share my goals with those people who have been huge role models for me. Many times, when I sent my goals to them, it was obvious that the stakes were high. One of the reasons I achieved those goals was that I didn't want to embarrass myself in their eyes. Sharing my goals with them brought us closer, and it drove me to work toward my best.

> "When performance is measured, performance improves. When performance is measured and reported back, the rate of improvement accelerates."
>
> —Thomas Monson

4. **Develop a plan and set milestones.** The next step is to develop a plan with milestones to accomplish your goals. Determine *what* you'll do in each step, with markers or milestones along the way. If the goal is to contact 300 potential customers by December 15, then you can break that down and set milestones such as making sure that you

contact at least three people a day for the next 100 workdays. Breaking down a goal into actionable milestones makes it doable. It's like using landmarks along the path of a marathon to mark your progress and keep you going.

5. **Post your goals in a prominent place.** The last, but very important step is to put your written goals and plan in a place where you can see them often. I suggest reviewing your annual goals or major goals regularly so that they remain fresh in your mind. It's frequently helpful to review them each week prior to doing your planning for that week.

Get a Leg Up with Goals

During my daughter Anne's junior year of high school, she shared with me her vision of playing soccer for a major university. She said she wanted to find a school where she could also earn a scholarship, receive a top-flight education, have a great team experience, and, last but not least, make great friends and maybe even meet a good candidate for marriage. That was the vision! My goal-scoring, goal-setting daughter developed specific goals to support that vision and went to work.

She set a time frame and milestones for contacting 10 university coaches by October of 2006 and giving them her credentials as an athlete. The idea was to begin the search process by seeing which schools might be interested in her.

Once several coaches had expressed interest in recruiting her, Anne planned visits to their campuses, setting up a matrix to provide a rating system for each school. Anne was very good about sharing all of her goals and plans with her mother and me, which we appreciated!

After narrowing her list, she visited her favorite campuses and talked to the coaches about their programs. Anne then received several scholarship offers. She used her original criteria to make a final decision, looking at those where she could receive a top-flight education, have a great team experience, make lasting friendships, and maybe even find someone to marry one day.

Anne weighed the options carefully. She asked our advice, but she ultimately chose the school that she felt best matched up with her goals. I'm very happy to report that she graduated from a PAC 12 university with a very useful degree, and that along the way she had a great experience on her soccer team, made friends for life, and, yes, found a wonderful young man who is also goal-oriented—in fact, he was the kicker on the football team.

Even though she had challenges along the way, her overall experience was very positive because she started with clear goals and a plan.

> "Good fortune is what happens when opportunity meets with planning."
> —Thomas Edison

Go for the Goal

My daughter is just one of the many people and organizations I've seen benefit from writing down goals and developing a plan to achieve them.

Figure 3.2 is an example showing how easy it is to write down your goals on a computer or a sheet of paper. You can modify this sheet to whatever works best for you. If you already have goals, I invite you to sit down this week and review them carefully. Is there a way to modify your goals and reflect a SMART perspective? If you haven't already written personal goals, I invite you to simply put pen to paper and try it this week. Determine your roles, develop significant SMART goals for each role, and send them to a handful of people who you trust and respect. The key is to take action. The art is in the start. You don't have to be great to start, but you have to start to be great!

My Personal Goals for _____
                                    Year

SMART (Specific, Measurable, Achievable, Relevant, Time-Specific)

ROLE:
Personal (Physical, Financial, Fitness, Emotional, Mental, Spiritual):

_____
_____
_____
_____
_____
_____

Family and Friends:

_____
_____
_____
_____
_____
_____

Professional or Student:

_____
_____
_____
_____
_____
_____

Community and Service:

_____
_____
_____
_____
_____

Accountability: I will share my goals with _____ and report on _____

FIGURE 3.2 Roles and Goals

Organizational Goals

In this chapter, we have so far focused on the principles for creating and realizing meaningful goals. Applying these principles in the business or organization setting is much the same.

The primary difference between personal goals and professional goals is that in business or organizational settings, goals and objectives are most successful when they are fully aligned with the vision and purpose of the organization and when they are shared with your key stakeholders.

When setting your goals, it is appropriate to answer the question, what is the greatest and most meaningful contribution that you can make in your organization?

You will be more successful when you are formally and frequently accountable for your progress. For example, you would not only set your annual goals, but also break down those goals into what you expect to accomplish each quarter. There is then an annual accountability and a formal quarterly accountability at the corporate or organizational level so that you can monitor your progress. This process helps to eliminate surprises and helps people to stay aligned with what matters most. Establishing this process for leading with a vision and managing with a plan (goals) helps you to stay focused day in and day out on the areas that are most vital for success and excellence within an organization.

In the beginning of this chapter, I mentioned that less than 10 percent of people have clearly written, actionable goals. Yet, we're nearly 90 percent more likely to achieve something when we have a clearly written goal. As a leader in your organization, you have a strong vested interest in making sure that your team members have clearly written and actionable goals.

Imagine the added value your organization would receive if each employee became fully engaged in the things that matter most to your success day in and day out. Not only that, but imagine your employees being more productive, more balanced in their work/home relationship, and less stressed because they know exactly what their focus and direction is. Roles and Goals provide your employees with a powerful and balanced approach to becoming more effective than they've ever been.

Let's move to the second part of managing with a plan.

Plan for the Unexpected

It's great to have a written and well-thought-out plan. Then again, how often do things actually go as planned? Not often, which brings us to another important consideration: planning for the unexpected.

As mentioned earlier, before each mission, my fighter pilot sons were schooled on the commander's intent, which gave them the guiding vision for their missions. They then developed very clear, measurable objectives (goals) to support the commander's intent. The next critical step was to develop contingency plans in case something went wrong—which it often does in their line of work.

What if the wingman has a problem with the jet over the ocean? What if the refueling tanker doesn't show up? What happens if there's cloud cover over the target? It's important to consider these "what-ifs" ahead of time rather than after they randomly appear.

The time to brainstorm isn't when your aircraft is hurtling through the air over the Black Sea and running low on fuel with lethal missiles tracking it. The same is true of your work and your life. Contingency plans are essential to your survival, yet they'll be much more effective if you think about your response before the crisis hits. Every leader needs to be prepared for health issues, changes in government regulations, product failures, lawsuits, a shift in the economy, and the loss of key people.

What's in your Playbook?

Sports offer great metaphors for life and business because we watch and understand the intricacies of the games we love. There are few better examples of contingency plans than the massive playbooks that football coaches put together to cover every possible development in a game. These coaches are masters of contingency planning because they know from experience that one play can turn the tide and render even the best game plan useless. They have to be prepared to pull out the playbook and respond immediately with a new strategy if there is an interception, a blocked punt, a fumble, a kickoff returned for a touchdown or a touchback, or any other game-changing shift.

This was demonstrated in abundance during the 2007 Fiesta Bowl game between underdog ninth-ranked Boise State University and eighth-ranked University of Oklahoma. The game was an absolute shoot-out with a series of stunning scores. Boise State seemed to be headed for an upset victory, but Oklahoma came charging late in the game, piling on 25 unanswered points and building a 35-28 lead with just 1:02 minutes remaining in the game.

It was a stunning turnaround in fortunes for his team, but with only 18 seconds remaining on the clock, the Boise State coach, Chris Petersen, pulled out his contingency plans and responded with three trick plays. The first was a wild and wooly play called "circus" in which a pass is thrown and the ball is then passed as a lateral to one of the open teammates.

Petersen's play allowed for as many as three laterals. In this case, one lateral was enough. BSU scored, and after it made the extra point, the game was tied at 35-35, sending the teams into overtime. Oklahoma didn't waste any time breaking the tie in the overtime period. The Sooners scored on the first play, moving ahead 42-35.

Once Boise State got the ball back, its team marched down to within five yards of the end zone and rolled out another trick play. For this one, the ball was hiked to the running back instead of the quarterback. The running back then threw in another trick by throwing the ball instead of running with it. The result was a touchdown pass to bring Boise State within one point, 42-41.

An extra-point field goal would have tied the game, but Petersen opted for a third trick play, a variation of the classic Statue of Liberty play in which the quarterback faked a pass and then handed off the football—behind his back—to a runner. The play worked. Boise State scored an additional two points and took the victory thanks to some very strong—and very tricky—contingency plans!

Do you think that Boise State was just lucky? Hardly. Coach Petersen and his staff had prepared for this type of contingency well in advance. They practiced and practiced the trick plays to perfection. The coach said that because of their many hours of practice, the team members had the stone-cold confidence to execute those plays successfully in front of millions of people and take an amazing victory against a determined opponent.

Having a contingency plan is critical to teams and organizations everywhere, but it also applies to you as an individual and to your family as well.

When you think about your contingency plans, one place to start is to consider what your first three responses would be to a crisis situation in your personal life or your organization. For example, if your spouse passed away, wouldn't it be helpful if you already had a place where family members could go for important information and contacts regarding finances, insurance, legal documents, and computer passwords? The mother of a friend passed away recently, and he and his siblings were surprised, but very grateful, to discover that she had left an updated will, detailed instructions for her burial and funeral, and the photograph that she wanted on her obituary. She also left a note for her grandsons saying that they would have to be her pallbearers "because I carried you all around when you were young, so now it's your turn to carry me."

Looking at contingency plans for your business, you should consider how you would respond to situations that could have a dramatic impact on your bottom line. What would you do, for example, if there were a product recall for one of your primary products? What would be your initial actions? It's not pleasant to think about some of these things, but if you do, like a football coach with a thick playbook, you'll be ready to respond when the unexpected hits.

When talking about contingency plans, the old adage rings true: "When the time to perform arrives, the time to prepare is past." Planning for contingencies, good and bad, can make an enormous difference to your long-term success and your efforts to become your best.

And now for the third and final factor in successfully managing with a plan.

Manage for Results

The first two steps have been all about developing the plan and thinking about contingencies; now we need to manage the plan for the optimal results. Leaders and managers are most effective when they are constantly striving to be their best.

A true leader goes beyond the status quo and inspires others to do the same. A true leader doesn't need to demand respect because others are inspired to follow the leader's example. Even with great plans, it still takes an effective leader to manage the plan and ensure that it is executed effectively. I invite you to think about your strengths and your areas for improvement to hone your leadership and management skills. Management skills can be applied both personally and organizationally, but no leader succeeds without building a strong team of individuals who share the same vision and goals. Let's look at the importance of building a strong team that supports the plan.

Develop Winning Teams

Even if you don't have the title of manager, you may need to enlist help from coworkers or family members to carry out your plan. Angela Wolf, the blind teacher, drew her students into her vision by making them her partners in the classroom. At the beginning of each school year, she explained what their relationship would look like. She was kind to them, and they committed to return her kindness by not taking advantage of her. In a sense, they became collaborators in her classroom, working together to achieve the best possible results.

Whether you're hiring people or trying to instill your vision into your current employees, you can't manage with a plan unless you make use of the talent around you. As Jim Collins would say, "It's not just getting the right people on the bus, it's getting them in the right seats."

The late Peter Drucker, a brilliant management expert, said that managers could be effective only if they "make people capable of joint performance, to make their strengths effective and their weaknesses irrelevant."

Your first question as a manager, then, is, "Who will help me execute the plan and achieve the vision?" You will need to harness a variety of resources to achieve your goals and be successful in executing your plan, but none is as important as the team that is working with you. Effective management means that you inspire and empower your team members to stand with you and help you succeed.

Once you've attracted good people and instilled the vision into them, you have to give them the freedom to respond to dramatic changes in the external environment. Decisive action may be essential during chaotic situations. There is rarely time to sit back and brainstorm, so your team has to have the confidence and the freedom to do what needs to be done in a crisis situation.

One of history's most powerful examples of the importance of an empowered team is offered by NASA's *Apollo 13* crisis, in which an onboard explosion crippled the spacecraft and endangered the lives of the astronauts aboard. The NASA command team had to scratch the moon landing and focus on getting the astronauts home safely. The new goal required a total team effort.

Under the calm, efficient, and heroic leadership and management skills of Gene Kranz, the lead flight director, the team went to work. Even though they had practiced a thousand times for similar contingencies, the people on NASA's team hadn't anticipated this particular problem. Yet they were prepared to find a solution.

Gene Kranz received many accolades for his performance during this crisis, but he is always the first to admit that he had a great group to work with. He set the vision and goals based on the new reality of their mission, with crew safety as the priority. He then kept his "White Team" (the media called it his "Tiger Team") on track, making needed adjustments along the way, until the new goal was reached and the astronauts were safely home.

How could this example of Gene Kranz and his team be helpful to you as a manager? If you haven't watched any of the movies, documentaries, or television mini-series about *Apollo 13* recently, I invite you to go back and watch and focus on Kranz's leadership and management skills.

In our seminars and training, we offer individual assessments and other leadership assessments. In addition, we have various self-evaluation exercises that focus on effective management techniques. The following is a simple self-evaluation tool for leaders and managers. It's beneficial for you to step back and evaluate yourself as a leader to identify your strengths and the areas where you need improvement. Reflecting on yourself, look at the following exercise and determine whether there are any areas that you want to work on. Rate yourself on these items on a 1 to 10 scale, where 1 = poor and 10 = excellent.

1. I motivate and inspire my associates, workers, or family members.

1	2	3	4	5	6	7	8	9	10

2. I recognize individual skills and potentials.

1	2	3	4	5	6	7	8	9	10

3. I bring out the best in my associates, workers, or family members.

1	2	3	4	5	6	7	8	9	10

4. I communicate well with my associates, workers, or family members. I am approachable.

1	2	3	4	5	6	7	8	9	10

5. I am a good, collaborative problem solver. I work to anticipate surprises in the external environment.

1	2	3	4	5	6	7	8	9	10

6. I am a good delegator.

1	2	3	4	5	6	7	8	9	10

7. I set clear boundaries and expectations.

1	2	3	4	5	6	7	8	9	10

8. I help associates, workers, or family members assume ownership of important tasks.

1	2	3	4	5	6	7	8	9	10

9. I am a good planner and priority setter. I clearly articulate the vision and goals together with my team.

1	2	3	4	5	6	7	8	9	10

10. I am continually working to improve my team and myself.

1	2	3	4	5	6	7	8	9	10

As you reflect on your answers to these questions, I invite you to choose the two areas in which you ranked yourself the lowest and then increase your focus on those areas in the weeks and months to come. As a leader, you are responsible for the success of the plan. Highly successful leaders are continually looking for ways to manage and lead their teams more effectively.

If you ranked yourself high in a few areas, great! Continue to accentuate those strengths. If there are some areas that need improvement, there is no better time than today to begin efforts to improve in them. It's about never being satisfied with where you currently are, but always looking for ways to improve as a leader and as an individual. That's the spirit of becoming your best.

Plan for Success

We've looked at ideas for becoming your best as a manager and a leader in business, organizations, and your personal life, which include:

1. Set annual goals using Roles and Goals and then develop a plan to achieve them.

2. Plan for the unexpected.

3. Manage for results.

Writer and philosopher Johann Wolfgang von Goethe said, "He who is plenteously provided for from within, needs but little from without." Who are the people who are "plenteously provided for from within"? They are those who are prepared with a plan. They know who they are, and they want to invest in something important.

The principles of "lead with a vision" and "manage with a plan" are the dynamic duo of peak performance. Whether they are applied personally, with another individual, or throughout your organization, these principles will consistently produce outstanding results and sustained, stunning accomplishments.

Leadership Action Steps

1. Remember that your vision becomes a reality as you develop a plan for achieving it.

2. Develop annual goals using Roles and Goals:

   - Review your vision and roles.

   - Set SMART goals.

   - Share your goals with someone you trust and admire to increase accountability.

   - Develop a specific plan with milestones for how to accomplish each goal.

   - Refer to your goals often.

3. Plan for contingencies in your personal and organizational plans. Always remember, "When the time to perform arrives, the time to prepare is past." Ask the difficult what-if questions now so that you're ready if a crisis hits.

4. Even with great plans, it still takes an effective leader to manage the plan and ensure that it is executed effectively.

5. Everyone can be a leader in some capacity. You don't need the title of manager to manage with a plan.

6. Take the simple assessment in this chapter to review your strengths and areas for improvement as a leader or manager. Continue to build upon your strengths, and choose the top two areas for improvement and identify specific actions you can take to improve in those areas.

CHAPTER 4

Prioritize Your Time

Do what matters most: start scheduling your priorities and stop prioritizing your schedule.

In February 1943, torpedoes from a German submarine exploded in the hull of the U.S. Army Transport (USAT) *Dorchester*. In a frantic effort to survive, the 902 soldiers aboard desperately searched for life jackets and lifeboats. Four U.S. Army chaplains, who were close friends despite their different religious affiliations, gave comfort and encouragement to the boys as they searched for life jackets.

The chaplains located life jackets in the storage lockers, put them on as many soldiers as they could, and guided those soldiers to the life rafts. When the final life jackets had been found and distributed to the soldiers, something nearly unfathomable happened.

Realizing that there were not enough life jackets, the four chaplains removed their own and fastened them on four terrified soldiers. As the *Dorchester* sank, the four chaplains stood arm in arm on the deck, singing as the ship disappeared into the sea.

Less than 30 minutes after the explosion, the USAT *Dorchester* had sunk. Thanks to the efforts of the four clergymen, 230 men were rescued.

FIGURE 4.1 (a) Chaplain John P. Washington;
(b) Chaplain Alexander D. Goode; (c) Chaplain Clark V. Poling;
(d) Chaplain George L. Fox

As this story illustrates, prioritizing what matters most occasionally means that someone must make a great personal sacrifice. You and I probably won't be called upon to make this kind of choice. Still, doing what matters most frequently requires discipline and maybe even sacrifices in your personal and professional life.

While the four chaplains went far beyond what most of us will ever experience, their story does illustrate a key point of guiding constant 4: we picture ourselves doing what matters most with our time in each of our individual roles. A chaplain's role is to save souls, and the vision the four chaplains had of their roles meant saving the lives of soldiers on the *Dorchester*.

This touching story is a reminder that our time on this earth can be cut short, and that it is short enough already for most of us. I have found that highly successful leaders think in terms of how they can do what matters most with their allotted time, whether at home or in the workplace.

Have you ever felt overwhelmed, or "task saturated," with phone calls, e-mails, interruptions, or competing responsibilities. Most people do feel swamped from time to time. It's a common lament in this fast-paced world.

We seem to have more tools for managing our time than ever before, but in spite of those tools, doesn't it feel as if the clocks run faster and faster every day? Overstressed and time-pressed people often attempt to deal with the strains by creating endless to-do lists and strict schedules, but at the end of the day, many people ask themselves, "Have I been doing what matters most?"

This principle is about time and how to do and become our best with the time we have in life.

This is about using your time to do what matters most instead of doing whatever is at the top of your to-do list. The time-management mindsets and practices that we share have helped improve marriages and family relationships. They've allowed many people to enjoy better physical, mental, and emotional health, not to mention improved productivity. They have helped individuals and teams within businesses and organizations maximize their productivity and achieve dramatically better results.

Time is still of the essence, just as Robert Herrick said back in the fast-paced seventeenth century:

"Gather ye rosebuds while ye may,
Old Time is still a-flying;
And this same flower that smiles today
Tomorrow will be dying."

The fact is that time and life can pass by all too quickly. What are you doing with the time that you have remaining? Benjamin Franklin wisely observed, "Do not squander time, for that is the stuff life is made of."

In our seminars, we've found that the material in this chapter has had more impact on participants than just about any other guidance we offer. It has transformed personal and professional relationships. It has allowed leaders and employees to look at their lives in a whole new light, enabling them to focus on what matters most without the stress!

Up to this point, we've looked at the value and importance of having a clear vision. After developing a vision, a person or organization should set goals and have a detailed plan to achieve that vision. This chapter is where the rubber meets the road, week in and week out. You will learn methods for transforming a poorly defined goal, like a typical New Year's resolution, into a real goal that's actionable.

Real success happens when you shift your focus from inaction to action by taking positive steps day by day during the week. You should always be asking yourself whether the actions you are taking each week are addressing what matters most.

As you read this chapter, imagine the effect that this material might have in your life or the life of a family member. Imagine the effect it would have in your organization if each of your employees always thought and acted in terms of what matters most while focusing on specific actions. Wouldn't that have a dramatic effect on the success of your organization?

Let's jump into it and look at three powerful actions that can help you stay focused on what matters most, personally and professionally.

They are:

1. Get your priorities straight and think HQ/HQ.

2. Take control of your life through pre-week planning.

3. Protect and conserve your time.

Get Your Priorities Straight and Think High Quality and High Quantity

The first action I recommend is all about doing what matters most so that you are focused on both high quality and high quantity (HQ/HQ). Think of a lens equipped with a prism made of your vision and your goals (see Figure 4.2). When you look through it, you can clearly see what matters most.

This lens brings into focus what matters most for you, your relationships, your work, and your impact on the world around you. The "do what matters most lens" helps you see and define your sustainable best, which is the opposite of a flash-in-the-pan best, a one-shot wonder, or a single shining moment.

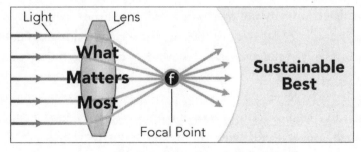

FIGURE 4.2 **This Lens Brings Your Goals into Focus**

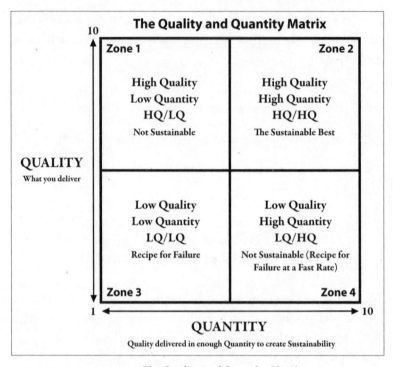

FIGURE 4.3 The Quality and Quantity Matrix

Viewing the demands on your time in terms of HQ/HQ (see Figure 4.3) helps you to focus on achieving sustainable excellence. When you have a focus on both high quality and high quantity, you are in the *high-performance zone* (Zone 2).

Let's say that a company's service technicians are so thorough and meticulous that they can make only one service call per day. The quality of their work is high, but the quantity—one service call per day—is insufficient. The service technicians must also attend to the *quantity* of work they complete if they want to remain employed. They need to complete enough service calls each day to generate the revenue needed to pay them and to provide an adequate return for their employer. If they don't balance a high level of quality and a high level of quantity, their jobs are not sustainable.

The same equation holds true in the personal realm. Parents who claim that they spend "quality time" with their children often discover that the quantity of time they spend with them is just as important, if not more important. The parent who has enough time for only an occasional "fun" outing with the kids may not score as many points with the family as the parent who is there for the kids in good times and in bad. Positive family relationships are difficult to sustain on quality time alone. There must also be quantity time. A balance of the two helps to foster closer bonds and more positive relationships. Individuals and organizations are most effective and successful when they reach the optimal HQ/HQ balance that puts them in the high-performance zone. What can you do to find the optimal balance? As Mahatma Gandhi said, "Speed is irrelevant if you are going in the wrong direction."

As you look at the HQ/HQ matrix, ask yourself which quadrant you're in, both personally and as an organzation. Personally, are you focused on HQ/HQ in your important relationships at home? Organizationally, is your product mix or service offering HQ/HQ?

If not, there's a possibility that what you're doing may not be sustainable over time. For example, if a company creates a large number of copies of a new product (high quantity), but finds that the product is flawed (low quality), that's a recipe for failure. Eventually someone will find a higher-quality solution.

If you're not in the high-performance zone (HQ/HQ), I invite you to sit down with a partner or a team and evaluate your plan. How do you need to adjust your plan to focus on what matters most? Maybe that means making adjustments as a parent. Maybe it means adjusting the development and production plan to launch a pilot rather than mass producing a product on the initial run.

This discussion of high quantity and high quality sets us up for a very specific way to focus on HQ/HQ by doing pre-week planning.

Take Control of Your Life Through Pre-week Planning

68% of leaders feel like their #1 challenge is how to prioritize their time. There's a common feeling of task saturation among managers and leaders around the world. For that reason, if I had to choose one thing out of all that we teach, this is probably the single most powerful tool.

Doctors and dentists have tools and instruments to help them perform their procedures. Firefighters, emergency and rescue personnel, teachers, plumbers, software designers, butchers, bakers, and candlestick makers all have tools that are specific to their trades.

Let me introduce you to a tool that can help you become your best in every area of your life. This tool can help you make your chaotic life more manageable because it focuses on scheduling your priorities rather than prioritizing your schedule. It does not involve creating an endless to-do list or a honey-do list, nor is it designed to track appointments. That's old school.

This time-management tool is designed to help you accomplish things that you may never have thought possible, by focusing on what matters most week in and week out, while increasing your flexibility and reducing stress in the process. That's new school!

The Power of Pre-week Planning

During their military training, my sons participated in an exercise called "Red Flag." During these exercises, there can be as many as 100 jets in the air, flying in close proximity as they drop live weapons on multiple targets. While they are doing this, they are also under mock attack by enemy fighters.

Before each mission, the pilots put in a significant amount of time planning the details of the mission to support the intent and accomplish the objectives. They call this *preflight planning*. What would happen if these pilots went out without a flight plan and just "winged it"? I expect that a lot of bad things would happen if they didn't have a detailed plan for that mission. Yet, as you look at your week, how many times do you go into the week and essentially say, "Let's see what happens this week"? How often do you just wing it and hope for a different result from the one the pilots would experience without a plan?

Like preflight planning, I've coined the term "pre-week planning." While you probably are not staging dangerous battles at 30,000 feet, your efficiency, flexibility, and stress management will significantly improve if you engage in careful and thoughtful preparation for what you'll do in the upcoming week. Pre-week planning is simple enough. You take 15 to 20 minutes on Saturday or Sunday and develop a detailed plan for the upcoming week.

I suggest Saturday or Sunday (assuming that is your weekend) because if you wait until Monday, the storm has already hit, and it will be too late for you to get ahead of the week. The time to do pre-week planning is when things are quiet and calm and you can spend a few minutes thinking about what matters most that week.

We typically find that people use either an electronic calendar or a paper planner to keep track of things, if they use anything at all. To help make pre-week planning as easy as possible, we've designed a Becoming Your Best planner. Although it's not necessary to use the tool, it certainly makes it easier. It is like hammering a nail, a person can do it without a hammer, but the tool (hammer) makes it a lot easier. If you want to use your own planner with this new mindset, you can adapt it, and that's fine as well. Do whatever works best for you.

Let's review the five steps to pre-week planning.

Step 1. Review your vision and your annual goals. This helps you put your week and everything that you're about to do in the proper perspective. As you plan your week, you can be thinking about what you should do this week to support the accomplishment of your goals.

Step 2. Look ahead one to three months, or even further out, in your master calendar. Is there anything you need to do this week to prepare for something that's still a couple of months away?

It is helpful to keep in mind that taking action today can prevent a crisis tomorrow. Ask yourself: What can I do this week to prevent stress and frustration in the future? For example, if you have a trip in three months, maybe you could book the airlines and hotel now to save time, money, and frustration later. Remember, action today will prevent a crisis tomorrow.

Step 3. Enter into your calendar all of the meetings and other scheduled events that you have planned for that week. Be sure to leave plenty of space between commitments to provide for flexibility and those many unexpected things that may pop up.

Step 4. Identify what matters most that week in each role. This is the most powerful step, and the one that's a game changer! This is where you bring your priorities into the picture. Now you should determine what matters most this week for each of your roles, whether as a leader, an employee, a spouse, a parent, or in organizations, clubs, and your community. In my case, I use the same roles for pre-week planning that I use in my annual goals.

As you reflect on each key role, stay focused on what matters most, giving priority to what is most important. Come up with two or three things that you can do this week in each role; however, if you have more than two or three things, that's fine.

This is a very powerful way to think about and plan your week because you're no longer simply reacting to what's happening to you. Instead, you are preparing yourself to do what is most important in each role of your life, and you are making time for it to happen. You'll find that you start doing amazing things in your various roles, things that you may not have thought about before. Now you won't have the excuse of saying that you didn't have time!

Here are a few examples of what you might come up with in some of your roles for the week. If you are a parent, you may want to schedule time to play a game with one of your children or spend a special evening together as a family.

As a leader, you may decide to take several of your employees to lunch to learn their stories, which builds trust and loyalty to your organization. As a salesperson, you may decide to contact a number of potential customers, write five follow-up thank you letters to key prospects, and call key customers who are having birthdays that week.

As a spouse, you can plan a date night or to leave a special note.

Earlier I said that we don't set New Year's resolutions; instead, we choose actionable goals. This is the difference! Use your goals as a guide during your pre-week planning. If you have a goal of going on two dates a month with your spouse, then you bring it to the weekly plan and make it happen this week. If your goal is to run a 5K in the next 60 days, then start preparing for the race this week by determining when and for how long you'll train!

This step elevates you to the high-performance zone. As you do this for each role, you should be thinking about what you *can* do this week rather than about what you *have to* do. It is a totally different mindset.

Step 5. Determine a time during the week when you'll do each item you listed under each of the roles. That way, you will have all your items scheduled, and you'll know when you'll do each of them. If taking your spouse on a date is what you'll do this week in the role of *spouse*, then figure out the day and time when you'll do it. You may need to coordinate a babysitter, so now you can plan when you'll do that as well. See how the things that matter most don't slip through the cracks anymore when you do pre-week planning? It's a conscious effort to focus on what matters most and then figure out a time during the week when you'll actually do it. It's where the rubber meets the road!

Once I am done with the pre-week planning, I generally sit back in a quiet place, think about the upcoming week, and look over the plan. I ask myself: *What have I forgotten? What can I do to be at peace and at my maximum effectiveness and efficiency? Is this week in harmony with my vision and my goals?*

Figure 4.4 shows a very simple example of what a weekly calendar might look like. You'll see the roles on top, and below them are those things that matter most to the individual. This is an example that was sent to me by a woman in California.

Whether you use an electronic calendar or paper planner, the process is the same.

It generally takes me between 15 and 20 minutes to complete my pre-week planning. Then I can enjoy the rest of the weekend,

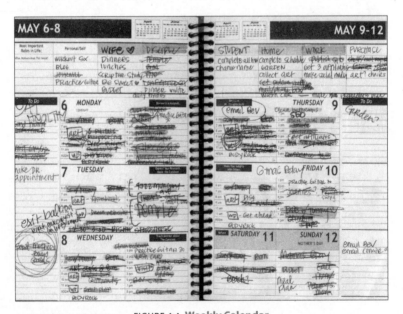

FIGURE 4.4 **Weekly Calendar**

knowing that I'm prepared for what lies ahead. Let me offer one more piece of advice that has proven valuable: once you've gone through your entire week, share your calendar and review your week with the people who are closest to you. If you are married, sit down with your spouse or your entire family and go over the week together. This ensures that your priorities align with your spouse's or your family's and that you are working together rather than competing with one another. This can save time and frustration later in the week. This practice also will help you avoid the inevitable conflicts, such as: "I thought *you* were going to take her to soccer!"

Pre-week planning is a powerful way to reduce stress, give you better quality time in each area of your life, and certainly increase your balance. It also prevents important things from slipping through the cracks. Of course there will be things that come up during the week that are urgent; then what? No problem. When you've planned your priorities into the week, there are certain things that you won't move because they are the things that *matter most!* However, every week you will need to make adjustments during the week. That's why this idea of pre-week planning is so refreshing. If a higher-priority item comes up, then you simply shift the lower-priority event to another day or time. Sometimes that may even mean moving it to the next week, but it will still get done.

The event that you shifted won't slip through the cracks or be forgotten. For example, if you were going to call a key client to wish him happy birthday at 10:00 a.m., but then your boss comes in and tells you that you need to complete a project by 11:30 a.m., you can simply shift the call to later in the day and focus on completing the requested project. The point is that the call will still happen because it's important and it didn't slip through the cracks. The result is a more loyal customer or client! The same idea would apply to every other role during the week.

We were holding a training workshop not long ago, and we were teaching this approach to planning. We used an example in the role of spouse, saying, "Leave a love note for my wife." One of the participants mentioned that if we had planned it, this wouldn't be spontaneous and it would not feel romantic or heartfelt.

The facilitator asked the participant how long she'd been married, and she responded, "Five years." The facilitator then asked her how many times she'd written a note to her husband telling him how much she loves him. The woman thought about it, then she sheepishly chuckled and said, "Never."

The facilitator pointed out that even if we plan something and put it on the calendar, it can still feel heartfelt and romantic—and it will get done. In this case, a note to the woman's husband would certainly have seemed spontaneous to him—after all, he'd never had a note like that from his wife. If you don't plan ahead, it might never happen!

I've seen this over and over. It's rare that we do these things that are so vital to our success and our relationships if we don't think about what we'll do and when we'll do it.

Keep in mind that this is a tool to help you realize your vision, your goals, and do what matters most. It is a framework that gives you a chance to remain focused even while under fire. This method allows you to make adjustments on the fly, on the run, and under the gun.

We've researched many methods for doing pre-week planning, from creating prioritized to-do lists to categorizing the events for this week and so on. Certainly each method has its place, but in working with highly successful leaders all over the world, we've found a process and a mindset that are very effective and that not only allow you to do what you need to do, but also help you think about what matters most in each important area of your life that week.

To further illustrate the impact of pre-week planning, let me share an example from a lady I'll call Jane. We'd visited with her off and on for months about planning her week and using the Roles and Goals format. She told us that she'd been meaning to have a special date with her daughter to celebrate her birthday, which had been in the fall. She was telling us this story in March, and she still hadn't taken her daughter on that special date. This was six months after her daughter's actual birthday. Jane said that time had simply slipped away from her and that she didn't get it done because she was "too busy"!

She knew that this wasn't right, and she wanted to try something that would help her take control of her busy schedule so that this potentially hurtful kind of situation didn't happen again. After we talked with her, Jane told us that she would give pre-week planning a try.

She went through the five steps that I just described, and over the next couple of weeks, she had a grand experience with her daughter, and with the rest of her family as well. I received a text from her after just two weeks saying, "I love this! It's the first time I don't feel stressed, and I'm accomplishing more than I ever thought possible. It's relatively easy, and it has made a huge difference. *Thank you, thank you!*"

Pre-week planning provides a laserlike focus that aligns your actions with your vision. It gets high-performance zone results. I was teaching this concept to the employees of one of the largest soft drink distributors in the world when one of the firm's executives caught my attention. I'd asked the participants to write down their primary Roles and Goals for the week. I asked a few of them to share their examples, and most of the executives talked about matters related to business. This one executive, though, wrote that his goal that week in his father role was to call his son.

He was a senior executive in his late fifties, so I found his words particularly interesting. I assumed that his son was no longer living at home. When I asked the executive for more details, he sadly reported that he and his son hadn't talked for seven years because of a long-running argument.

While doing the exercise in our workshop, the father realized that what really mattered to him in that role was reconnecting with his son that week. I encouraged him to do that.

He agreed, but he said that it would take him some time to prepare emotionally.

I checked back with him when I returned for a follow-up session a few months later.

"Did you call your son?" I asked.

"Yes, and it went very well," he said. "In fact, we couldn't even remember what we had argued about seven years ago. Now, we're talking at least once a week. I am so glad that you helped me look at what was truly important in my life so that I could put everything else aside and go after it. I found that having a better relationship with my son flowed over into making me a better person all the way around. I've found that I am more successful at work by having my whole life in order."

I regularly visit with top salespeople in my work and my travels. I ask these top performers why they are consistently among the best. They tell me that one of the most important things that helps them to be highly successful is planning ahead and setting goals concerning how many people they will contact that week, when they will contact them, and whom to contact, meaning who the best potential customers or clients are.

That is pre-week planning at its best—and they follow through by doing the work they've scheduled. This process and mindset may not protect you from challenges that arise that are beyond your control, but it does give you a foundation for focusing on what matters most to you week in and week out.

If you would like a planner to help you get started with pre-week planning, simply go to www.BecomingYourBest.com and visit the store, where you can invest in a world-class electronic or paper-based planner.

Figure 4.5 reminds you how easy the most important steps of pre-week planning really are.

I invite you to choose a time during the next weekend when you can take 15 or 20 minutes and try this idea to see how it works out for you. Then do it consistently for three months and see what the impact is on your life and the lives of those you care about. Imagine the effect it might have if everyone on your team approached each week this way! Imagine the

FIGURE 4.5 **Pre-week Planning**

effect it might have in your personal life and the effect it might have on your family. You have nothing to lose by trying this experiment.

Let's now move to the third and last way to prioritize your time and do what matters most.

Protect and Conserve Your Time

The sheer speed of daily life can spin you away from what matters most. In a world in which everything seems urgent, it's easy to feel hammered from every side by things that are not that important to you or your business.

We are bombarded by instant communication and information thanks to the Internet, smartphones, e-mail, and social media. Filtering out what is important is a growing challenge, and one that is increasingly vital to your success. To stay focused on what matters most, you need to create internal guidelines so that you don't get trapped by all the distractions. Those less important things that can dominate your time must be tucked into their proper place so that you can take care of what matters most.

Let's talk about specific things that you can do to protect your time.

Handle It Once

This is a phrase that is familiar to my family. My wife, Roxanne, has hammered it into every cell in our bodies. It is her motto. We have talked about it in family meetings, she has put signs all over, and it is one of the best time-management tools that exist.

The point is to handle each task when it arises and not procrastinate. Make the bed first thing in the morning. Read your mail when it arrives. Do the dishes after dinner. Resist the temptation to say, "I'll do it later." If you procrastinate, important things tend to get pushed back.

Manage Your E-mail and Other Electronic Media Effectively

This doesn't mean that you should ignore electronic media. E-mail is an extraordinary communication tool when it is used correctly. You simply need to stay on top of it to help you achieve what matters most.

You may be in a profession where it's critical that you respond to e-mail or voice mail in a timely way. We each need to know when to use e-mail or voice mail. If an item is emotionally charged, hard to communicate, a key negotiation, or better handled in person, don't e-mail. Handle it face-to-face if possible, or in a phone conversation.

E-mails and voice mails are best used for transactional communication or for the exchange of information. Have you ever felt tempted to respond to an emotional e-mail when you're fired up? Resist the urge. It's rarely the correct response. When your negative emotions are high, it's best to cool off, then respond in person or on the telephone. To prevent e-mail or voice mail from distracting or overwhelming you, set aside a specific time period each day to read or listen and then respond to it. You might consider silencing or turning off your e-mail or voice mail notification tool, then setting aside two or three blocks of time during the day to handle it.

Have you ever watched a person respond to every little ding his phone makes, or have you even been that person? There has to be a better way! The worst part is that most of the e-mail that is flowing in is either junk or spam.

I recommend using filters to screen or block the spam and junk e-mails so that you don't waste time on them. If you work to strike a balance between controlling the time you spend on e-mail and ensuring that you communicate in an effective, timely way, you'll control electronic media instead of letting them control you. So, be determined to develop and practice good e-mail and Internet-perusing habits.

Try to Eliminate or Minimize Ineffective Meetings

Another thing you can do to conserve and protect your time is to avoid wasting time in meetings that don't accomplish anything. Sometimes the best meeting is the meeting that you don't have. Don't meet unless you really need to!

If communication is informational and doesn't require responses or deliberation, then there is no need to have a meeting. In fact, if the information can be communicated in some way other than in a meeting—in an e-mail or by telephone, for example—I'd suggest trying those options first. When conference calls or meetings *are* necessary for collaboration purposes and to maximize communication, consider the following ideas:

- Invite only those who need to be there.

- Have an objective and meaningful purpose for the meeting.

- Start on time and be on time (or preferably a few minutes early). Encourage everyone who is attending to be a few minutes early so that people aren't walking in after the meeting has begun.

- Have a clear agenda, and provide any supporting documents or reports ahead of time.

- Make a record of issues and decisions.

- Invite participation. If participation is unnecessary, you shouldn't be meeting, so send the information another way.

- Create a "parking lot" for items that surface but are not appropriate for the current meeting. Put these items on a future agenda or handle them later.

- During the meeting, prevent any single discussion from taking too much time.

- Close with a review of any action items for individuals or the group.

- Schedule when and where the next meeting will be.

- End on time or early. Do not go past the designated time to end the meeting unless something critical comes up.

- Make a habit of taking your weekly planner with you. Then if you find yourself stuck in an ineffective meeting, you can use the time to reflect on what matters most, record ideas for each of your roles, and plan for actions that will help you achieve your goals.

I make it a goal to leave meetings inspired, one way or the other—even if I have to inspire myself!

Avoid Negative, Draining Interactions with Others

Recently, a close friend—a very capable individual—called and wanted to know if he could come over and visit with me about an important matter. He had just had a run-in with a neighbor, a local church leader, and he wanted to discuss what to do. As my friend and I talked, we developed a plan to help resolve the issue and restore good feelings. When my friend returned home, the neighbor was on his doorstep; both were prepared to apologize and get back on the right foot. They had a nice 45-minute conversation during which they resolved things and restored a high level of trust. They are both capable, very intelligent, high-achieving individuals.

The initial negative interaction that started the whole thing probably took only about 45 seconds. Then they each went their separate ways, stewing over the unpleasant interaction and unresolved issue. It took about three hours to resolve the issue and restore good feelings. Working together, they figured out how to resolve the issue that had caused the problem in the first place. All of the ill feelings were forgotten, and they both moved forward feeling good about the resolution.

I have had similar experiences. Wouldn't it be much better to completely sidestep these types of events in the first place? It would save valuable time and emotional upset. Avoiding these types of negative interactions might save you hours, days, or even weeks of worry and strife.

> "You live longer once you realize that any time spent being unhappy is wasted."
> —Ruth E. Renkl

Remember that negative interactions, confrontations, and altercations with others can sap your energy and strength. To help you diffuse negativity, try the following:

- Avoid negative interactions in the first place. Anticipate possible conflicts and figure out how to eliminate them before they come up.

- Tap into your inner strength based on the guiding constants. When you feel your blood beginning to boil, take a deep breath and make the decision to take the high road so that you can find a positive resolution.

- Keep things in perspective. Do you really have to solve the problem right away? Can you tell a humorous story to break the ice and then work it out?

- Figure out a way to communicate better and to deal with issues before they become a challenge.

- Be quick to listen and slow to wrath. Practice the steps to effective communication discussed in Chapter 7.

- Try to avoid individuals who are chronically negative or inclined to drama and "blowouts." Life is too short.

You can't really change or control others, so don't allow them to throw you off. Draw upon your strong inner core for your own peace, happiness, and direction. Your positive and peaceful energy and your effective use of time are two of your most precious resources. Be a master at conserving them carefully.

Priotize Your Time and Do What Matters Most

In this chapter, I've covered three actions that can help you do what matters most. They are:

1. Get your priorities straight and think HQ/HQ.

2. Take control of your life through pre-week planning.

3. Protect and conserve your time.

I hope this chapter has inspired you to reflect on how you use your most valuable assets: your time and talents. Are you doing what matters most in your personal life, with your family, in your organization, and in your community? Certainly we can all do better and improve the use of our time to leave a legacy of greatness. I invite you to try pre-week planning and see what difference it might make in your life. It's a powerful tool that has helped thousands of people take control of their lives and their busy schedules. As I mentioned in the beginning, of all the things we discuss, this has been one of the most significant game changers in my life personally.

This is the magic of the 12 principles and how they tie together. It's the reason that those who aspire to be highly successful leaders find ways to make these principles part of the culture of their organization and also incorporate them as habits in their personal lives. Highly successful people create a vision, develop goals and a plan to accomplish their goals, and then focus on what matters most through pre-week planning to make the goals a reality week in and week out. I encourage you to apply these principles and processes in your journey to become your best!

Leadership Action Steps

1. Develop a "what matters most" mindset.

2. Start scheduling your priorities and stop prioritizing your schedule.

3. Take time each week to carry out pre-week planning:

   - Review your vision and goals. What can you do this week that helps you accomplish your goals?

   - Look out at the next several months on your master calendar.

   - Determine your roles and what matters most this week in each role.

   - Find a time to do what matters most during the week.

4. Work to achieve sustainability by balancing high quality and high quantity, both personally and as an organization.

5. Keep yourself ahead of the curve by scanning your long-term calendar regularly. Remember, action today can prevent a crisis tomorrow.

6. Protect and conserve your time and positive energy through good organization and a clear lens on what matters most.

7. Use e-mail, voice mail, and other communication devices effectively and wisely.

8. If you hold a meeting at all, make it productive and worthwhile. Don't waste others' time!

9. Visit the store at BecomingYourBest.com to invest in a new Becoming Your Best planner for you or your team.

PART TWO

Transformational Teams and Relationships

**12 Principles of
Highly Successful Leaders**

12 Never Give Up!

1 Be True to Character

11 Live in Peace and Balance

2 Lead with a Vision

10 Apply the Power of Knowledge

3 Manage with a Plan

9 Be Accountable

4 Prioritize Your Time

LIVING

LEADERSHIP

TRANSFORMATIONAL

TEAMS AND RELATIONSHIPS

8 Innovate Through Imagination

5 Live the Golden Rule in Business and in Life

7 Be an Effective Communicator

6 Build and Maintain Trust

CHAPTER 5

Live the Golden Rule in Business and in Life

Treat others right in business and in life.

My family was on the final leg of a 120-mile dream vacation when the cold, cruel world interrupted our reverie. We'd been mesmerized by incredible views of mountains, waterfalls, and a spectacular countryside during this South American journey. Our trip had begun on a boat, but as we traveled from Bariloche, Argentina, to Puerto Montt, Chile, we switched to a bus.

After our driver had stopped a couple of times to let people off in the villages along the route, a German couple suddenly jumped up and yelled first in their own language, which I couldn't understand, and then in English: "They've stolen everything! They've taken all of our money, our passports, everything!"

The bus driver pulled over so that everyone could search for the couple's missing backpack. The Germans were distraught. They didn't have enough cash to make a phone call. They spoke no Spanish. They appeared to be devastated, and I couldn't blame them. Anyone who has traveled abroad has experienced "passport panic," in which even the thought of losing those vital documents can send you scrambling from your bed and making a frantic search.

In this case, the German couple had lost not only their passports, but their credit cards and IDs as well. They were scheduled to begin a cruise the next day, but they'd lost their tickets, too. Without proper identification, they'd never even be allowed into the port.

I empathized with our fellow travelers. The thieves could have targeted us just as easily. Watching their panicked conversation as they tried to figure out what to do, a thought hit me: *I have about $200 in my wallet, and we're leaving for home this evening.*

I pulled the woman aside and offered to help, asking how much they needed. After checking with her husband, she said, "We need $500."

The price of helping was steeper than I'd thought it would be. After a brief conversation with my family, we pooled all of our money and found that we had a total of $540. We decided that we could get to the airport and make it home with our credit cards and $40 in cash for our taxi to the airport.

I did have some misgivings. My first responsibility was to take care of my wife and children, but if there was some sort of emergency, I still had my credit cards. I also had some concern about handing over our cash to strangers, but losing $500 would not have been a long-term threat to the family finances.

Two considerations set the course for our eventual decision. First and foremost, I asked myself: *What would we want someone to do for us in that same situation?* Second, we decided that if we really wanted to help, we couldn't worry about seeing our $500 again.

So, I gave the couple most of our cash reserves and bid them good luck. I had no idea whether we'd ever hear from them again, although they did ask for our contact information. I needn't have worried. After returning home, we received this e-mail from our new German friends:

Dear Steve,

I am writing this email from Puerto Natales to say thank you so much for the confidence you showed us by giving us money without knowing us. I am expecting my husband back today from the embassy in Santiago de Chile with a new passport. We had a difficult time, and needed many phone calls and rearrangements to get a new passport for him. The police were not helpful at all; they let us sit in the police station for several hours.

We will arrive back in Germany on January 19. I will transmit the $500 US to you then ASAP.

We would also like to invite you and/or your family to our house should you or your kids ever be visiting Germany. We live close to Heidelberg and some more nice places which are worth a visit. Our son went to school for one year in the U.S., and my husband is traveling a lot in the U.S., so we would be really happy to welcome you.

They repaid the money, and we all felt good about the experience. I was especially proud of our children, who had stepped up immediately and offered their cash to help the strangers who'd been robbed. This experience is one that we'll remember for the rest of our lives. Through this experience, a great friendship was forged.

It's one thing to know the Golden Rule and another to live it. I find this especially true in the business world, where the drive for profits and growth can become so dominant that the concept of serving others gets lost. However, while living the Golden Rule day to day in the business world may be challenging, many people have discovered that it pays unexpected dividends. One of those dividends is customer loyalty, a valuable asset in any enterprise.

Studies have shown that the probability of selling goods or services to a new customer is only 5 to 20 percent, while the probability of making a sale to an existing customer increases to 60 percent or even 70 percent. If you aren't living the Golden Rule and treating your customers right, you run the risk of never creating a solid customer base. It is much more expensive to constantly be chasing customers than to serve those who are loyal to you. The average company loses 10 percent of its customers each year. A 5 percent reduction in your customer defection rate can significantly increase your profits, depending on the industry.

The lesson here is that the Golden Rule isn't just a noble goal in business. It is good business—and it is beneficial to the bottom line. Most successful business leaders and companies with enduring brands have learned that treating customers right is vital.

A Rule for the Ages

The spirit of the Golden Rule, simply put, is to "treat others as you would like to be treated." Studies have found that this is considered a "golden" standard for living for good reason. For centuries, it has been viewed as an ideal for civil human interaction. Scholars have found mentions of this humanistic approach to life in writings from Egypt more than 3,500 years ago. The essence of this rule is found in nearly every religion, including Christianity,

Hinduism, Judaism, Islam, Taoism, and Buddhism, and in the ancient Greek philosophies. The rule transcends time and culture and can be a game changer when it comes to your long-term success and relationships.

Even though the Golden Rule has stood the test of time and has been embraced by philosophers, religious leaders, and other great leaders, most people would agree that in our complex, fast-paced, and global society, it is more often cited than followed. It's much easier to do unto others as you would have them do unto you when you are face to face and eye to eye. However, in today's world, human interaction is increasingly done via the smartphone, over the Internet, or by text and Twitter.

Personal communication is too often impersonal. We interact and do business with people we may never meet face to face except on social media. Governments, businesses, and organizations make decisions that affect millions of people who have no vote or even a voice because they live miles from the decision makers, maybe even on the other side of the planet.

Before the dawn of high-speed interstate highways and commercial jetliners, travel provided ample opportunities for cultural interaction and Good Samaritan moments of kindness and grace. Today, however, interaction between fellow passengers on commercial flights is rare. On the road, we drive vehicles with tinted windows that provide anonimity and make it all too tempting to cut in and out of traffic, bump bumpers, honk horns, and make threatening gestures. The number of drivers who are suffering from road rage often seems greater than the number of those who follow the rules of the road.

The Golden Rule Counterpoint

There is a counterpoint to the Golden Rule, of course, and it can provoke a negative ripple effect that is both powerful and damaging. I was once on a commercial passenger plane that was stuck at the gate with no air conditioning on a very hot day—even hotter on board.

A fellow passenger was making things even more uncomfortable by raising a stink because he wanted to move to first class. The flight attendants wouldn't allow it, and this resulted in even more obnoxious and rude behavior on the part of this person. He continued to complain and carry on for several hours after the flight took off. If someone had suggested buying him a parachute, I might have chipped in and escorted him to the door.

At the arrival gate, he threatened to write to the president of the company and report everyone on the crew. The one positive thing he did was to unify everyone else on board. We all agreed that he was a pain to travel with. The ripple effect he caused was ugly for everyone. It made air travel less appealing to us all, but, hopefully, it made most of us determined to never act so badly ourselves.

We can choose to become embittered by such experiences, or we can resolve to use them to make ourselves better. I chose to see this man's bad behavior as an aberration because everyone else on the plane was very patient and good-natured. You can't turn sour on the entire human race because of a few stinkers. If you immerse yourself in kindness, you may well come to see the world as a kinder place.

You Reap What You Sow

The Golden Rule is related to the law of the harvest. The premise of this law is simple: you reap what you sow. Here's how it works: Do you want to receive justice and fairness? Then be just and fair in your dealings with others. Do you wish that others would notice that you need help and then help you? Then recognize those in need and assist them.

One of our neighbors, Carolyn, told me about a recent traveling experience that gave her a new perspective. She was at the airport and was next in line while waiting for the skycap. She heard the passenger in front of her berating, belittling, and yelling at the skycap. The angry passenger was in a hurry and was very impatient. The skycap finished with the passenger, and as the passenger left, Carolyn stepped forward.

The skycap turned to her with a warm smile and asked how he could help her. Carolyn said, "How can you be so pleasant? You just got abused by that passenger."

The skycap smiled and said, "That man is going to New York City, and his luggage is going to Israel! Now, how may I help you?"

You can believe that she practiced the Golden Rule with that skycap. He had retaliated against the previous passenger's rudeness with a strong message of his own. The traveler had treated him rudely, and he had responded in kind by sending the traveler's luggage on a trip of its own!

If you are inconsiderate, you may well get back what you dished out, in heaping helpings. But if you dish out kindness, you are likely to reap rewards. In talking about the Golden Rule, a friend of mine offered this comparison, "Throw your bread into the water and it comes back toasted and buttered." It's something of a mystery how this law works, but it is true. Somehow what comes back to us is almost always more than we send out.

I have found that in the business world, and in any other type of organization, employees will go to the ends of the earth to do a great job when they know you also care about them and their welfare.

Living the Golden Rule in a genuine way produces significant returns for you. You will have more peace. You will feel more confident and satisfied with your life. Your opinion of yourself will improve, and you will feel capable of accomplishing all of your goals and dreams. However, these "returns" on your investment of time and means are not the reason that you decide to be a person who helps others.

We Are All Fellow Travelers

It can be an impersonal world, but we are all fellow travelers on this planet. It is no coincidence that across many cultures, the mythical and real heroes of our stories are often those who practiced the Golden Rule. In the same way, the most celebrated, beloved, and successful leaders throughout history—including Abraham Lincoln, Mahatma Gandhi, Mother Teresa, and Nelson Mandela—have embraced the concept of treating all men and women as they would want to be treated, in other words, treating people right. They applied the Golden Rule and changed the world.

None of them were perfect human beings. You don't have to be perfect either, but I believe that living this principle in your daily life, at work and at home, will help you to become your best. Every single day, I experience successes and also failures when it comes to living the Golden Rule. I try to improve each day, and that is something that I recommend to you as well. I am excited to suggest four very significant ways that you and I can apply this ageless rule in our modern world. Those suggestions are:

1. Use the power of kindness.

2. Be caring and give service to others.

3. Put others first—and take them all the way home.

4. Four powerful tips to live the Golden Rule.

Let's look at each of these suggestions in more depth.

Use the Power of Kindness

It's not about a single act. This is a mindset of serving others and going out of your way to help and empathize with those in need. We reap what we sow in business and in our personal lives, and this is the way to reap many rewards. Among the greatest of those rewards is the ability to inspire others to pass on acts of kindness.

There may be times when living the Golden Rule doesn't seem natural and takes more effort—as if you are checking off an item on your to-do list. When the Golden Rule becomes more reflexive and instinctive, you will feel transformed.

It's helpful to decide in advance that you will look for opportunities to be of service and suspend judgment—both of the people you might help and of their circumstances. As you do these things, you develop the selflessness that is at the heart of living the Golden Rule. It becomes more natural to be a source of kindness if you look for opportunities to reach out.

One of my favorite examples of this involves another travel story and a man who I knew and admired greatly. A severe storm had caused delays and flight cancellations at Chicago's O'Hare Airport. Thousands of stranded or delayed passengers were impatient, cross, and irritable. Among those who were in trouble was a woman, a young mother who was standing in a long line at the check-in counter. Her two-year-old child was on the dirty floor at her feet, and she was pregnant with another child. She was sick and obviously weary to the bone.

Several people looked at the wayward child and his sickly mother with disdain. No one offered to assist her. Then my friend approached with a kind smile and an offer: "Let me help you."

He lifted the dirty, crying child from the floor and held her warmly in his arms. He gave the toddler a stick of gum to calm her. Then he asked for assistance and helped the mother and child move to the front of the line. He even spoke with the ticket agent, and he soon had her checked in.

This Good Samaritan then found seats where she and her child could be comfortable, chatted for a moment, and disappeared into the crowd without giving her his name. I know that my friend would prefer not to be identified, but I can tell you this: he was the leader of a massive organization and had many responsibilities. He could easily have ignored this woman's plight with the excuse that he did not have time for her.

Another friend was with him when this took place. This example of kindness and empathy had a great impact on his life and the way he treated others. I wonder how many other people in the airport were positively affected by this display of kindness—how many thought, "The next time, I want to be the person who steps up and makes a difference."

Acts of kindness can be contagious, you know. I read of a similar incident involving a woman whose husband was serving in Afghanistan. She put a bumper sticker on her car that said: "1/2 my heart is in Afghanistan." After coming out of a restaurant, she noticed $40 on the seat of her car with a note that said, "I noticed the sticker on the back of your car. Take your hero to dinner when he comes home. Thank you both for serving, him while deployed and you for waiting. God bless! (signed) A United States Veteran."

This was a simple act, yet after this woman posted the note on social media, there were more than six million views and thousands of comments. As I read through the comments, I was amazed at how many people said they were going to find a way to do something kind for someone else because they were inspired by this one simple act.

Think of the ripple effect! That single act reached around the world.

Are you and I constantly looking for opportunities to lift those around us and make the world a better place? Don't you think that would be a great way to live? What effect would it have on your work environment or in your home?

If you're in a place where you can write, I invite you to take a pen or pencil and write down some acts of kindness that you can do for others, whether they're simple things or more elaborate. I encourage you to follow through so that you can experience the rewards and the joys of giving to others.

Be Caring and Give Service to Others

I've been associated for many years with a company that has been highly successful in applying the Golden Rule to its business practices. Synergy is a business that promotes efficient and renewable energy. When it was founded about 30 years ago, Synergy's leaders established a vision that declared in the company motto: "We Treat People Right"!

That vision has guided every member of this firm in the treatment of both employees and customers. At the very heart of this motto is a desire to live the Golden Rule by caring for and serving those who are involved in the company and its customer base.

Over three decades, Synergy has grown to be a market leader in its industry. In a recent company annual retreat, its leaders reaffirmed that "We Treat People Right" will continue to guide the business. The company's customer service department offers a special opportunity to shine as an example of the Golden Rule in each interaction. Almost regardless of the reason for the complaint, its goal is to astonish customers with immediate and extraordinary service.

Not long ago, a customer who'd had energy-efficient lighting installed in his home more than seven years earlier called to say that there was a problem with it. His two-year warranty had expired five years earlier, but Synergy's policy is to serve its customers' needs in order to promote goodwill and protect its reputation. The company responded by making sure that all of the customer's lighting was working and in perfect condition. He was quite pleased at the high level of service and responsiveness. As a result of this experience, the man wrote a letter to the utility companies (Synergy is a customer of the utility companies) to express how grateful he was for Synergy's prompt service. In turn, this significantly increased the trust level between the utilities and Synergy.

Synergy receives few complaints, so the cost of responding to them and addressing them is minimal. It has come to see any expenses in that area as investments in goodwill and the best investments in the future of the business that the company can make. Of course, the company follows through and troubleshoots each complaint with a goal of eliminating them altogether.

Synergy's customer service has become legendary in its industry. One of the benefits of incorporating the company motto as a business practice is the opportunities created for building goodwill that affects the overall success and vitality of the company.

Put Others First—and Take Them All the Way Home

Living the Golden Rule is a higher way to exist, a way that many people might find incomprehensible. It can provoke amazing responses in a world that often seems driven by selfishness rather than selflessness. This struck me when I learned that a simple act of sportsmanship had become a multimedia sensation and a source of inspiration around the globe.

In 2008, teammates Mallory Holtman and Liz Wallace of Central Washington University's softball team carried injured opponent Sara Tucholsky around the bases so that she could finish scoring her first career home run, even though both CWU players knew that it could cost them the game (which it did). Two other players were on base, so three runs were scored as a result of their Good Samaritan act, helping to eliminate their team from the NCAA championship tournament.

CWU may have lost out in its playoff bid, but the university and its players earned national accolades, and there were more than a few tears when Mallory and Liz reached out to their opponent so selflessly. The opponent, Sara Tucholsky, playing for Western Oregon University, tore a ligament in her knee as she rounded first base after hitting the softball over the fence. The umpires ruled that if a pinch runner came in for her at that point, she couldn't advance beyond first base. While coaches and umpires debated about the NCAA softball rule, Holtman and Wallace applied the Golden Rule.

Their act of sportsmanship, which brought tears to the eyes of many witnesses, was honored and praised across the country thanks to replays on YouTube and ESPN, which gave the CWU players an ESPN ESPY Award (Excellence in Sports Performance Yearly). Holtman later told reporters that she and her teammate helped Tucholsky without giving much thought to how her scoring might affect the outcome of the game because, "It was just the right thing to do."

This is a wonderful example of highly successful leadership in action. It's so refreshing to read about someone who lives the Golden Rule, especially an athlete who rejects the "winning is everything" mentality and instead lives for the greater good. The story of two softball players reaching out to an opponent in need should inspire you to emulate the generosity, fairness, and service to others demonstrated by those athletes who lived the Golden Rule.

What's interesting about this dramatic example is that it arose naturally and without any expectations. Many of your own opportunities to help others may come when you least expect them. Will you be ready to respond in that moment of choice?

Imagine what would happen if your coworkers had this mentality. What impact would that have on the morale in your company? What would it do for customer loyalty and turnover if your company developed a culture of caring and finding special ways to serve customers? Imagine what the impact would be if your employees were to address all of your customers by their first name or simply greet them with a smile and warm hello. What would be the long-term impact?

These small acts of kindness result in significant deposits that can pay huge dividends over time. To help you live the Golden Rule in your daily life, at work, and at home, I've included some suggestions in the next section.

Four Powerful Tips to Live the Golden Rule

Before I review these four powerful tips for living the Golden Rule, permit me to touch on an important point. At its core, living the Golden Rule is not dependent on how others treat you. Instead, it is a fundamental mindset and condition of the heart. It is how you think of and treat others. If you're a business leader, it's what you develop as a culture in your company. Ironically, because of the baggage that can build up in close relationships, you may sometimes fail to apply the Golden Rule with those who are closest to you as much as you do with strangers. But it should be applied to everyone!

When you are living this "rule," you should not expect reciprocal treatment. You should give freely and generously, without concern for what may be returned to you. To presume a quid pro quo removes the "golden" aspects of this principle. Sometimes it's intuitive to live the Golden Rule. Other times it helps to have a plan when you see opportunities. Now, let's review the four tips for living the Golden Rule.

Tip 1: Carry a Shield of Love

From time to time, sometimes even daily, we will encounter people who are offensive, rude, thoughtless, unkind, and sometimes downright mean. One of the best ways to respond to a person or situation like this is with love.

A couple of humorous, but very effective ways to counter these types of fiery darts is to have a defensive arsenal of love.

Try this one out and see how it works for you: when someone is unkind or less thoughtful than he should be, say to yourself, "I love you, and I forgive you." This is extremely powerful. Countless sales representatives find this to be a great tool as they talk to people each day.

Make an effort to love someone, even when that person has been mean or rude to you. Yes, this is difficult. It's counterintuitive. However, just watch the peace, power, and control that come into your total being as you take the high ground and respond with kindness guided by this force field of love.

These actions allow you to be friendly, to smile, and to be kind and considerate at every opportunity. You will feel better, and so will the people around you. You may not change the other person, but you will create a better situation, there is a chance that the outcome will be more positive and productive, and you will feel better in the process.

This type of discipline and control also helps while you are driving. If you encounter someone who is a thoughtless, aggressive, dangerous, or rude driver, you may apply the same type of response, stay in control of your emotions, and end up in a safer place. You can always report dangerous drivers to the authorities, but you will not get dragged down to their level of behavior.

Tip 2: Empathize with Others

We all tend to get caught up in our own concerns, problems, and feelings. As a result, we can become desensitized to the needs of others. The Golden Rule is a reminder that you should be as attuned to the people around you as you are to yourself. Viktor Frankl recalls, "We who lived in concentration camps can remember the men who walked through the huts comforting others, giving away their last piece of bread. They may have been few in number, but they offer sufficient proof that everything can be taken from a person but one thing: the last of the human freedoms—to choose one's attitude in any given set of circumstances."

Tip 3: Be Compassionate with Others

When you feel critical of another person, consider saying to yourself, "There, but for the grace of God, go I." Then offer compassion instead of judgment. Often, you don't know why someone may be doing what he's doing or why he's acting the way he is. It is better to err on the side of kindness and compassion than that of judgment and criticism.

Tip 4: Celebrate Differences and Avoid Prejudice in Every Form

> "Speak not injurious words neither
> in jest nor earnest. Scoff at none
> although they give occasion."
> —Sixty-fifth of George Washington's Rules of Civility

Prejudices can easily become ingrained in our perceptions of others. Make it a habit to celebrate the differences of others. Look at each individual as a fellow human being with unique skills, talents, and abilities that you can learn from, regardless of that person's background, skin color, faith, attractiveness, height, education, gender, or age.

> "We have committed the Golden Rule to
> memory; let us now commit it to life."
> —Edwin Markham

Go for the Gold

This guiding constant, "Live the Golden Rule in Business and in Life," is one of the most defining principles of highly successful leaders, and of highly successful lives as well. We have discussed multiple ways in which you can live the Golden Rule.

1. Use the power of kindness.

2. Be caring and give service.

3. Put others first—and take them all the way home.

4. Four powerful tips to live the Golden Rule.

As you incorporate these thoughts and ideas into your life and your business, you will be happier, and so will the people around you! As the great poet and writer Maya Angelou noted: "I've learned that people will forget what you said, people will forget what you did, but people will never forget how you made them feel."

Leadership Action Steps

1. Living the Golden Rule is a principle of conduct taught in virtually every country, every culture, and every religion.

2. Living the Golden Rule is a call to set aside your self-interest and reach for something higher.

3. "You reap what you sow!" What you send out, personally or professionally, will eventually come back to you.

4. We are all fellow travelers on this earth. How do you treat others? How do you treat others when they can do nothing for you in return? These are questions that you should ask yourself often.

5. What is the ripple effect of your actions? Whether you treat others with respect or you are mean to others, you will leave a ripple effect. Determine now to leave a ripple effect of kind deeds and acts. Improve the world where you stand today by leaving a wake of kindness. Leave a note, change a tire for someone, pay for a stranger's meal at a restaurant, give a homeless person a sandwich, and so on.

6. The probability of selling to a new customer is between 5 and 20 percent, while the probability of selling to an existing customer increases to 60 to 70 percent! Find a way to treat your customers right so that they come back to you time and time again.

7. Carry a shield of love in your life. It's so much more powerful than hate and anger.

8. Be compassionate with others.

9. Avoid prejudice. Look at people as fellow human beings and treat them accordingly.

10. When all is said and done, those who are close to you will remember you by how you made them feel.

CHAPTER 6

Build and
Maintain Trust

*Create dynamic teams and relationships
that get winning results.*

This principle is like a reservoir. In building a reservoir, a location is chosen, then a dam is designed and constructed. Once the dam is finished, the river slowly fills the reservoir. The process can take years.

Once it is completed, a reservoir creates energy that can be used hundreds of miles away. However, if the dam isn't built and cared for properly, it can fail, with catastrophic results. In most situations, if the dam were to suddenly break, the water would drain within a few hours, flooding the surrounding area.

A well-built reservoir becomes a major asset, providing energy, recreational opportunities, and beauty to a region. When properly maintained, it can usually withstand flooding, earthquakes, and other potential threats. The power, strength, and potential for good in a reservoir serves as a metaphor for business and personal relationships built on trust—both for you as an individual and for society in general.

Like a reservoir, trust takes a long time to build, but if it is broken, the reserves you've built up can be gone in an instant. When there is trust between two people, their relationship can usually withstand challenges like disagreements and misunderstandings, but if the reservoir of trust is low, even small problems can cause serious damage.

Think about the relationships you have that are very trusting. You are probably grateful for them because you don't have to put a lot of thought and energy into them. Then think about those relationships that aren't built upon trust, either because they are relatively new or because of something that makes trust difficult. These relationships often consume more of your time and energy, which makes them difficult to maintain.

Trust and Be Trustworthy

We use the words *build* and *maintain* in the title of this principle because those words imply that trust is something that the highly successful leader constructs over time and then nurtures over the course of any relationship, whether it is with a family member, a coworker, an employer, or the community. Strong and deep relationships are built upon trust and trustworthiness. When you betray a trust, it shows a weakness in your character, and that leads to fewer opportunities and diminished chances for success.

When you do things that increase the level of trust, your capacity to build relationships, create and seize opportunities, and achieve success increases substantially. When trust is high, you become more effective and influential in all aspects of your life. Even the most complex interactions and transactions become significantly easier when there is a high level of trust.

The Simplicity of Trust
I once owned some land in a mountain community. When I decided to sell it, I approached a friend, Scott, who owned quite a

few of the lots in our small community. We had developed a close relationship over the years, and we trusted each other.

I told Scott about my interest in selling my lot and asked him if he was interested in purchasing it. He inquired about the price. I gave him my offer, and he countered with an offer that was lower than I was willing to accept. I told him that I had invested money to improve the property and was hoping to at least get that investment back out of the property. So, I countered with an offer that fell somewhere in the middle. He took a few seconds to think about it, then agreed to the price.

The entire transaction took about 90 seconds. In the weeks that followed, we probably spent another 15 or 20 minutes total to handle all the paperwork. That transaction took place more than four years ago. We've both been delighted with the deal. This transaction for a substantial piece of property was simple because of the high level of trust we shared. If there had been a low level of trust, the transaction would have consumed more of our time and energy as we worried about being taken advantage of.

Certainly I would have been more careful with someone I didn't know and trust so well. This is why trust is so pivotal to the success or failure of an organization. We all prefer to do business with those we trust.

Imagine what the result of low trust might be for a team, family, business organization, or military unit. Would you like to be an astronaut in space who doesn't trust the engineers and officials on the ground at the control center? A commercial airline pilot who doesn't trust the air traffic controllers at the airport? An international businessman who can't trust his suppliers thousands of miles away?

How important is trust in your life? Do you spend enough time building and nurturing it with those you love, do business with, or interact with regularly? A July 1999 *New York Times*/CBS News poll revealed that 63 percent of those interviewed believed that "you can't be too careful" with most people in business dealings. In fact, 37 percent believed that "most people would try to take advantage of you if they had the chance."

If you want to influence, do business with, or interact safely with others, building trust is essential. How do you build trust? The same poll revealed that 85 percent of respondents expect the people they "know personally" to try to be fair. Could it be that simple? Let people see who you are, help them feel that they know you, and your trust ratio with them automatically triples. Think about things you've undoubtedly heard: "He's okay—I *know* him," or, "It's not that I don't trust her, I just don't *know* her."

There are three specific things you can do to build and maintain trust.

1. Evaluate trust in your relationships using the Trust Meter.

2. Build and maintain trust through your actions.

3. Learn the stories of those around you.

Evaluate Trust in Your Relationships Using the Trust Meter

Imagine that you're driving alone at night, in a desert with no gas station for 100 miles, and you look down and see the gas gauge at full (see Figure 6.1).

How would you feel and act if you saw the gauge on full? You would probably feel content, confident, and at ease. Really, you probably wouldn't have to worry about it!

On the other hand, imagine in your mind's eye that you are alone on that desert road, and

FIGURE 6.1 Gas Gauge at Full

when you look down, you see in horror that the gas gauge is on empty and the fuel light is on (see Figure 6.2).

FIGURE 6.2 Gas Gauge at Empty

How would you feel and act? You might feel panicked and stressed. You might wonder how far you will have to walk. All your attention and energy would be focused on the gas gauge. Basically, it would be a miserable situation to be in!

Let's compare your relationships to the gas gauge and instead call the gauge a "Trust Meter." Imagine each of your important relationships, whether it's with a partner, a child, a parent, a coworker, an employee, or a customer. Is the trust level in your relationships closer to full, half a tank, or empty? As you consider your relationships, note that if the Trust Meter is low, then that relationship can consume a great deal of time, energy, and worry—sometimes leading you to neglect other relationships or essential activities.

When your relationships are built on a high level of trust, the Trust Meter is on full, which allows you to use your time and energy in much more productive ways and places. Why is it important that you maintain the Trust Meter on full with those in your organization or business? People may give you their business simply because they trust you. Your competitors might have a less expensive product, or maybe even a higher-quality product, but customers may choose you because they trust you more than they do your competitors. This is one of the reasons that I tell people that trust can be the million-dollar difference!

If you are trusted, people will generally be relaxed around you. They will be confident that you will treat them well and fairly. That's one reason why trust can be an important economic factor in your business and why you and I should always be striving to move the Trust Meter to full. You can insist that people follow you, but you can't insist that they trust you.

Look at each of your relationships using the Trust Meter as an evaluation tool. If the Trust Meter isn't full, whether in your personal life or in your business, it would be wise for you to figure out what you can do to move the needle to full. You may be tempted to wait for the other person to respond, but I recommend that you take the initiative to improve the level of trust. This evaluation of your relationships then takes us to the next question: What are specific actions that you and I can take to build and maintain trust?

Highly successful leaders build high levels of trust with consistent, deliberate, and thoughtful actions.

Build and Maintain Trust Through Your Actions

You certainly want to trust others, and you want others to feel that they can trust you. Often, people know what needs to be done to increase trust, but actually doing it is a challenge. Other times, it helps to hear some fresh ideas on how to create a more trusting relationship. Here are a few specific actions you can take to make yourself worthy of trust:

- Do high-quality work and finish it on schedule. If people say they'll do something by a certain time and they don't do it, the level of trust usually drops. I encourage you to do high-quality work and either finish it on time or let the other party know that it will be late.

- Be consistent so that others will see you as reliable. Consistency will build trust in all your relationships. Do what you say and say what you'll do.

- Be predictable. Have a reputation for following through on what you say you will do. Return phone calls and respond to e-mails on a timely basis. Be responsive.

- Be open in communicating commitments, and be willing to have your performance measured. Communicate your intentions and motives so that your actions are transparent.

- *Give* trust. As with most other things in life, you get what you give. Giving trust often results in returned trustworthiness.

- Tell the truth. If you are hiding something or telling half-truths, eventually you will get caught up in your web of lies, and this will drive the Trust Meter down. For inspiration, look at a list of large companies that suffered when trust was violated. Enron and WorldCom are just a couple of examples. When people find you trustworthy, they'll prefer to deal with you. Opportunities for growth and progress come to those who are trusted.

As you achieve trustworthiness and meet the expectations of others, you will experience peace and balance in your life. Your relationships will be more rewarding, you will be better able to resist negative influences, and you will build self-respect.

Conversely, when you are not trustworthy, you are more likely to view others as being untrustworthy—and you may behave selfishly and cynically by "getting them before they get you." Because trust is reciprocal, you develop it by developing your own trustworthiness.

When you are trustworthy, you develop another capacity at the same time: you develop the ability to trust yourself. Trust creates greater self-confidence.

When you trust yourself:

- You trust your inner voice.

- You trust in your competence, and you are secure enough to listen to and measure all input.

- You trust in your character because you have the power that comes from consistency.

Remember: Trusting yourself is often a prerequisite to trusting others.

Business Applications: Establish Organizational Trust

Another specific action you can take to build and maintain trust includes conscientiously working to establish trust at all levels of your organization.

- If you're an employee, do you trust your supervisors?

- If you're a supervisor, do you trust your employees and feel that they trust you with their concerns?

Workplace frustration is one of the top reasons why people quit their jobs. How many of those frustrations could be solved by having a higher level of trust and better communication? When people get frustrated, they tend to hold it in until it comes to a boil. Would this happen if there were higher levels of trust inside our organizations and if people felt that they could share their real concerns?

With that in mind, what's the process in your family or organization for sharing concerns or ideas? What if there's a sexual harassment issue in the office, or a product defect, or any of a number of other things that could really hurt the company? Is there a high enough level of trust and a process in place to allow the employees to discuss it with their supervisors?

Be careful of falsely assessing situations. We've often found disparities between how supervisors feel and how their employees feel when it comes to trusting each other. That is a recipe for a lot of frustration!

Trust doesn't simply flow from the top down. It's vital that you have a culture in which employees are willing to share their feelings, to express concerns, and to offer solutions. For that to happen, highly successful leaders create a culture of listening and understanding the ideas and feedback from others, no matter how unpleasant the circumstances may be. These are the characteristics of high-trust relationships. This is what they look and feel like.

Trust Can Save Lives and Companies

The experience of 10-year-old Tilly Smith and her family illustrates a powerful example of this. In December 2004, they were vacationing on Phuket Island, a part of Thailand. While they were enjoying a walk on the beach near their hotel, Tilly noticed that the seawater appeared to be receding. It was calm on the surface, but there were so many bubbles that foam began to appear.

Tilly had just learned about tsunamis—powerful and destructive waves caused by earthquakes and other disturbances—two weeks earlier in school. She recognized the calm, but frothy and receding waters as classic warning signs that a tsunami was approaching. She immediately told her parents and her sister that a tsunami was coming and that they had to get to higher ground. Her father alerted the hotel security, but her mother was slow to react.

Tilly insisted that they leave for high ground right away. Finally her mother followed. Security officials cleared the beach. Minutes later, a tsunami hit. The father trusted his little Tilly. Because of that trust, they helped save the lives of more than a hundred people. An estimated 270,000 others perished in that tsunami.

Tilly's geography teacher later said that the power of education might mean the difference between success and failure, and also between life and death. In this case, Tilly's family knew that they could trust her because of her knowledge and confidence. Because they trusted her, they acted upon her warning, and their lives were spared.

- What would you do if you were on a beautiful beach and a hysterical 10-year-old ran past yelling, "Tsunami!"?

- What if others had hesitated in responding to the 10-year-old girl's warnings?

- What is the role of trust in this scenario?

Tilly trusted her training. She was so sure of her knowledge that she broke away and ran; others trusted her and followed. Those who didn't listen and trust her put themselves at great risk.

Let's relate this to your business or organization. How many good ideas are floating around inside your organization, but not acted upon? Maybe one of these ideas could make the difference between the long-term success or failure of your organization.

Do supervisors and coworkers trust employees enough to listen to their ideas? Are you willing to listen to others and trust them, no matter what the impact of the information might be? This can be critical if there is a problem with a new product or if there are reports of sexual harassment, for example. It takes a high level of trust for supervisors to listen and act upon employee input, especially if it is highly technical or complex.

It is difficult to give and receive trust if it has not been established based on past behavior. A company's customer service center serves as a sort of laboratory to show the impact of trust and the lack of it in the business world. When a customer service team finds out that customers are upset, team members can take this as an opportunity to demonstrate the company's core values and actually increase customers' trust.

What follows is an adaptation of some customer service apologies that I found in a blog post by marketing guru Seth Godin, in which he describes various ways companies respond to customer complaints. He graciously gave me his permission to share a few of his examples. The first few invite mistrust. The later examples demonstrate how trust can be built. As you read each example, think about how you might respond.

Customer Service Call Responses

RESPONSE 1: "You can always take your business elsewhere."
CUSTOMER: "Thank you, I will, and so will all my friends."
RESULT: Trust plummets.

RESPONSE 2: "It's not our fault."
CUSTOMER: This is not an apology; the company wants to play the victim.
RESULTS: Frustration and withdrawal of trust.

RESPONSE 3: "We're sorry you feel that way."
CUSTOMER: This is not an apology. Roughly translated, the company is saying, "Your feelings are your problem. It bothers me that you feel that way. If you didn't feel that way, I would be happy."
RESULT: Trust drops.

RESPONSE 4: "I'm sorry if we did something wrong."
CUSTOMER: The company is apologizing without acknowledging responsibility.
RESULT: No trust established.

RESPONSE 5: "We're sorry that we let this happen."
CUSTOMER: This sounds like an apology, but what will the company do to make it right?
RESULT: A step toward trust, but a very tenous one.

RESPONSE 6: "We're so sorry that we caused this problem. Please know that we take this very seriously. This is a huge oversight on our part. I will immediately notify my supervisor, and we will review our procedures to ensure that this cannot happen again. In the meantime, that is no consolation to you for our lack of service! What can we do to regain your trust? We will be sending you a little surprise as a token of our appreciation of having you as a customer."

CUSTOMER: The company is taking my complaint seriously and
   acting upon it.
RESULT: Trust established and built.

Build Customer Relationships Through Trust

I have been associated for many years with a company that per-
forms energy-savings audits and services for homeowners and
small business owners. One of our customers said that his air con-
ditioner wasn't working properly, and that he was unhappy with
us. Even after we performed a tune-up service, the unit wasn't
blowing out cool air.

So here's what our company did. One of our associates visited
with the customer so that we could understand the problem in
detail. Next, our technicians arrived within hours to correct the
problem. Finally, one of our team members delivered a gift and
reviewed the customer's feelings about the service to make sure
that his expectations were met.

We didn't just talk about what was right. We followed our
company's mission statement and did what was right. By the time
we left, the Trust Meter was on full. Our challenge as a company is
to have our service fill the Trust Meter to full the first time around.

Reach Out to Your Customers and Contacts

I may have been around long enough to be considered an "old
school" entrepreneur, but the basis of this guiding constant is
embraced even by the latest generation of highly successful leaders. The *Washington Post* reported that in 2014, Facebook founder
and chief executive Mark Zuckerberg challenged himself to write
one thank you note each day. The young entrepreneur, who was
just 19 when he established Facebook in 2004, had grown sensi-
tive about his reputation for being critical of people, especially his
employees, so he is making an effort to build and maintain trust
by being more appreciative of those around him.

Zuckerberg is not alone in seeing the value of this, by the way.
Douglas Conant, former CEO of Campbell's Soup Company,

told the *Post* reporter that during his 10-year tenure with that major food brand, he has written at least 30,000 thank you notes to connect with employees. Conant said that he takes at least an hour a day to write thank you notes to employees who have done well. He recommends the practice to other top executives, who can tend to overdevelop their critical "muscles."

With that endorsement from two top leaders, let me briefly share three powerful ways to build trust and enhance relationships both inside and outside an organization:

- Increase customer "touches." Your clients and customers should know you and be familiar with you. By "touches," I'm referring to the number of times you interact with a customer in positive ways. The more personal you can make it, the better. For example, you can send personalized thank you cards with handwritten notes to key clients or partners. How many businesspeople do that in today's busy world? It might also mean sending clients gifts or discount coupons on their birthdays or during special times of the year. The point of doing this is to build trust. When customers feel that there is a personal connection, they are more likely to continue doing business with you.

- Reach out to your team. If you're a leader, try writing notes to your employees thanking them for their sacrifice and hard work. Praise your employees in these notes, and express your appreciation for their contributions. Think about what that would do to build the trust and loyalty of your people.

- When talking with clients or customers, find something in common with them. This may sound simple, but all too often I hear people making pitches or launching into business without taking the time to connect on a personal level. Establishing common ground or shared interests that build bonds, whether it's similar backgrounds, shared hobbies, or having kids who play the same sport, can pay huge dividends. Remember, if they know you, they're more likely to trust you.

- Respond to e-mails or calls in a timely fashion. How do you feel when people don't respond to you? Whether or not you respond in a timely manner will certainly affect the needle on the Trust Meter.

Those simple steps can help to increase trust in any organization. Anyone can do them, it just takes a little time and conscious effort. Leadership expert Warren Bennis says that trust is the major leadership challenge of today and tomorrow. Trust is crucial to every happy and successful relationship; everything you do in life is built on trust. A high level of trust makes it easier to solve even the most difficult of problems. A low level of trust makes it difficult to solve even some of the easiest problems.

You can build trust by being kind, exercising patience, listening, completing tasks, consistently delivering results, returning phone calls or e-mails on a timely basis, and doing what you say you will do. When the Trust Meter is full, you feel strong and confident in your relationships. But when the Trust Meter is low or close to empty, your relationships can become seriously strained. When the Trust Meter drops to empty, family or business relationships can die.

One final, yet very powerful way to cement trust with other people or organizations is to get to know them well enough to understand what motivates and inspires them.

Learn the Stories of Those Around You

I attended a conference and workshop on customer relations in which an executive from the Chick-fil-A fast food chain talked about the value of building trust by getting to know the people who are involved in your business dealings. The company had taken a stand on a number of social issues. This had become a tense and awkward public battle. Many people were picketing various Chick-fil-A locations.

This executive from Chick-fil-A arranged to sit down with some of the protestors, but he didn't have high hopes for a positive resolution. There was a great deal of trepidation associated with this meeting.

As they sat down, the Chick-fil-A executive asked one of the principals from the picketing group about his background and how he'd become an advocate for his cause. He appeared to be sincere in his interest, so this potential adversary responded with sincerity. The picketer said that he'd lost his father 16 years earlier, when a drunk driver had killed him in an accident. He then gave a brief history of his involvement in his cause.

The Chick-fil-A executive said that he was grateful for the man's taking a few minutes to share his story. The executive said that he too had lost his father to a drunk driver, 30 years earlier. In sharing their backgrounds, the two potential adversaries had established a common ground, which is where trust begins. They made significant progress regarding the issues at hand and agreed to work toward shared goals.

The first step in creating bonds of trust is to build a rapport based on shared experiences and mutual understanding. It's difficult to work with someone you don't trust, and it's even harder to trust someone you don't know. The challenge in this fast-paced and hectic world is to learn the stories of those around you in order to build bonds of trust with them. Highly successful leaders always find a way to build relationships.

To build trust with someone, try these four game-changing words: *What is your story?* Some people have worked in the same organization or industry for months, years, or even decades and really don't know one another. No matter what your profession may be, if you take the time to get to know the people around you, it will establish a higher level of trust and foster opportunities for more business.

My son recently tried this while traveling on an airplane. He turned to the stranger who was seated next to him and asked him a few simple questions about where he was from and where he worked. Their conversation continued for an hour and a half. The passenger told my son that he *never* talks with fellow passengers on planes. Yet when my son asked him about *his story*, a bond was created—one that continues to this day. A couple of hours after they landed, our son received an e-mail thanking him for that time and conversation. In fact, the former stranger, who also happened to be a CEO, said that he might use our training company's services—all thanks to a connection built on trust.

If you're a supervisor, do you know the stories of those who work with you and for you? If you're an employee, do you know the stories of your supervisors and those whom you work with? Once we really understand each other, we can appreciate and trust each other at higher levels. If you're in sales, remember that most often, people aren't paying only for the product; they're investing in a trusting relationship with you and your company. If they trust you, they're likely to listen to you and buy into your advice. Think about this: if you're in sales and you take a few minutes to listen to each contact and learn about his or her background, chances are that at least some of them will respond by wanting to know more about you, which helps build bonds and trust.

In our seminars, we have fun with this idea. We have people pair up and share information about themselves. Participants are often surprised at the connections they can establish because of shared backgrounds or interests. Even if they've known each other for a long time, they often discover new commonalities that strengthen their bonds.

I encourage you to invest your time in getting to know others at every opportunity. Listen attentively, and share your story too once you've heard another person's. You may be surprised at the result of being a good listener and creating bonds of trust. Of course, your goal is to learn all you can about the other person without that person feeling that he or she is being interrogated.

I invite you to get to know at least one new person each week, or to make the effort once a week to learn more about somebody you already know, with no goal other than to learn more about the individual. The rewards of doing this can last a lifetime.

Build and Maintain Trust

In this chapter, we've discussed three powerful methods that highly successful leaders consistently use to build and maintain trust personally and within an organization:

1. Evaluate trust by using the Trust Meter.

2. Build and maintain trust through your actions.

3. Learn the stories of those around you.

NASA Apollo astronaut Alan Bean (see Figure 6.3) said, "I had to trust a team and they had to trust me to get me to the moon. And the size of that team was 256,000 people. And I trusted them. And they got me to the moon."

FIGURE 6.3 *Apollo Spacecraft*

Whether it is a team of 2 or a team of 256,000, there is great power in trusting relationships. Ralph Waldo Emerson once said, "Trust men and they will be true to you; treat them greatly and they will show themselves great."

As you work to become your best in your relationships and your career, trust is a critical component. I encourage you to build trust through consistent, deliberate, and thoughtful actions, and may you enjoy the happiness and success that comes from well-earned high-trust relationships.

Leadership Action Steps

1. How does the Trust Meter look in your relationships? Is it nearly full, half a tank, or empty? What can you do today to move the needle on the Trust Meter to full?

2. Be trustworthy and loyal, especially to those who are absent.

3. There are certain actions you can take to build trust. Do what you say you'll do, and if it's going to be late, let someone know. Return calls and e-mails. Be predictable. Do high-quality work. Tell the truth.

4. Establish trust at all levels of your organization. You never know when a game-changing idea will surface. Ideas are more likely to surface when there is a high level of trust between supervisors and employees.

5. The ultimate measure of trust transcends legal documents and agreements. Trust is a matter of character and commitment to the well-being of everyone in balance with becoming your best.

6. Build on common ground. Trust is established when you get to "know" someone.

7. As an organization, increase customer "touches." Write personalized thank you cards, call key clients or friends on their birthdays, and so on.

8. Ask people this magical question: "What's your story?" Listen intently and learn about them. When you learn about someone and what makes that person who he or she is, trust tends to go up dramatically.

9. Trust is a commitment to:

   - Be dependable.

   - Give and receive feedback.

- Show respect.

- Demonstrate humility.

- Remove hostility and anger.

- Be thoughtful.

- Make and keep psychological agreements.

- Listen to understand.

- Build character.

- Demonstrate competence.

- Say, "I'm sorry."

- Be counted on.

CHAPTER 7

Be an Effective
Communicator

Listen carefully and practice restraint of tongue and pen.

Back when my wife, Roxanne, and I had four boys under the age of nine keeping us on our toes, she announced that despite her heavy workload at home, she wanted to run a marathon.

My wife has never lacked energy or ambition.

On the other hand, I had taken a vow many years earlier that I would never punish my body by competing as a marathon runner.

But for some reason my sound thinking flew out the window, and I heard myself saying, "Sure, I'd be happy to run the marathon with you."

The next thought that hit me was: "Did I really say that out loud?"

I made the commitment, and Roxanne held me to it with a vengeance.

In truth, however, although my feet and knees may not agree with me, running that marathon turned out to be one of the greatest experiences of our lives.

To prepare for the marathon, we undertook and completed a 16-week training program. This regimen helped us to become more physically fit, and it also provided us with rare one-on-one time to talk and share our feelings.

It also gave me the opportunity to become a better listener. One morning on a training run, I asked Roxanne how she was doing.

"Fine," she said.

Her tone was not what you'd call blissful and carefree. She sounded a bit stressed. Normally, I might have let it go, but I'd been researching the art and power of listening. I sensed that there were emotions behind the "fine" that weren't so fine.

"That didn't sound like a very convincing 'fine,'" I said.

Her next comment just about knocked me over.

"Actually, I've never been more discouraged in my whole life," my wife said.

Whoa! I thought. *This is not the time to make light of her words, or to try to solve any problems. I'd better focus on just listening.* Besides, I figured that she might knock me off the road and into the ditch if I didn't shut up and listen.

"It sounds like things are really weighing heavily on you," I said.

For the next 20 minutes, my wife unburdened herself of something that had been troubling her. I didn't interrupt, which proved to be a wise move. By the time we finished our run and reached our front porch, my wife's mood had lifted. She gave me a hug and said, "Thank you for just listening. I didn't really need any advice. I just needed someone to listen. Thanks for letting me verbalize my thoughts."

And then she went into the house, leaving me on the front porch with a deeper appreciation for the power of listening. What was especially amazing was that Roxanne felt much better, and the issue that had been troubling her never came up again.

Was I tempted to jump in and offer my thoughts and solutions while she was venting? Of course! But I'd learned that what my wife really wanted to do was express herself. She wasn't looking for solutions at that time. She was trying to sort out her feelings.

If I had given in to temptation and tried to interject my thoughts and feelings, I can guarantee you that my wife would not have been as happy with me as she was when we reached home. I often tell participants in our seminars that being a good listener is one of the greatest gifts we can give to those we care about—and to ourselves as well.

> "Listening is a magnetic and strange thing, a creative force. The friends who listen to us are the ones we move toward. When we are listened to, it creates us, makes us unfold and expand."
>
> —Karl Menninger

Look at Your Own Communication Style in Business and in Life

Consider your relationships and how you respond to your spouse, your children, your employees, and your customers when they come to you with a concern. How well do you feel you listen? Do you focus on their words and the emotions behind them? Do you hold off responding until they've finished and you have a full understanding?

Has anyone ever told you that you could be a better listener? Being a great listener is a rare quality and one that takes considerable effort. Some of the most successful people I know also happen to be great listeners. In the business world, the art of listening and effective communication can make the difference between success and failure.

There also are helpful and important guidelines to master when your job as a listener is done and you take your turn as the speaker. One of the primary rules of great communication for the speaker is to be clear and concise.

My sons often talk about learning this in their training as military pilots because imparting unclear, overblown, or incorrect information during a flight mission can be deadly. The same holds true in other branches of the military and in civilian life, too, of course. After a mission, pilots conduct a debrief, in which they assess the effectiveness of their communication.

Clear communication that flows both ways is critical, both in business and in relationships. Companies that have open lines of communication with their employees report that their workers are more engaged and perform at higher levels. According to communication consultant David Grossman, retail giant Best Buy reported that higher employee engagement scores led to better store performance. For example, for every percentage point that they boosted employee engagement, individual stores saw a $100,000 increase in operating income annually, he noted.

Grossman also estimated that businesses in the United States and England lost an estimated $37 billion annually as a result of employee misunderstandings (including actions or errors of omission by employees who had misunderstood or been misinformed about company policies, business processes, their job function, or some combination of the three). He surveyed 400 corporations in that study, and he also found that the cumulative cost per worker per year of productivity losses resulting from communication barriers is $26,041. That's significant! Certainly the amount of damage done depends on the industry and the company, but what if you were losing $26,041 a year per employee because of communication issues? Wouldn't that be worth changing?

The Keys to Understanding

In working with executives and other leaders around the world, I've found that one of the biggest challenges many of them cite is effective communication—whether it's internal communication between employees or departments, or external communication with suppliers or customers. As a result, our clients are always looking for ways to improve their communication, but few of them realize that better communication begins not with speaking or expressing yourself, but with *listening* to others instead.

One of my favorite quotes about listening comes from an unknown source but rings very true: "The greatest mistake we humans make in our relationships; 'we listen half, understand a quarter, think zero, and react double.'"

How you listen to others says a great deal about your character. So, to become a better listener—a sincere, interested, positive listener—you must begin with what's inside of you.

The intellectual, poet, and writer Oliver Wendell Holmes Sr. once noted, "It is the province of knowledge to speak, and it is the privilege of wisdom to listen." I've also heard it said that the greatest compliment you can pay someone is to truly listen. Think about the people you value as mentors and guides in your life, and you'll probably realize that one of the things you value most about them is that they are willing to listen to what you have to say.

Thankfully, with effort and practice, we can all become more effective communicators and better listeners. Let's look at four steps toward that goal:

1. Be a highly effective communicator.

2. Avoid communication roadblocks.

3. Master the art of feedback.

4. Learn to control your emotions.

Be a Highly Effective Communicator

For most of us, it can be a real challenge to listen with empathy, which means to listen with the goal of understanding the emotions that are being expressed as well as the words that are being said. If you've ever been in a difficult conversation in which the other person said, "You're not hearing what I'm saying," it is likely that you weren't listening with empathy. You were probably listening with the goal of finding a solution or resolution rather than simply trying to understand the person's feelings as well as his words. Whether we're talking about a personal relationship in the home or landing a $100,000 business deal, understanding the other person and being a highly effective communicator can make all the difference in the world. Let's look at some of the keys to becoming a highly effective communicator; as you read them, ask yourself how you're doing right now with each step, both in your personal and in your professional life:

> **Look the person in the eyes.** To help stay focused during a conversation, I make a point of looking into the person's eyes and identifying the eye color. I've observed salespeople at trade shows, and I can always tell the true sales professionals from the others because they make steady eye contact. The less professional salespeople tend to let their eyes wander during conversations and pitches, which is a surefire way to lose a sale—and future sales.

> "You cannot truly listen to anyone and
> do anything else at the same time."
> —M. Scott Peck

> **When someone is speaking to you, don't worry about what you're going to say next.** Attempt to focus on each word the person is saying. If you concentrate on what is

being said, you are less likely to miss nuances and important messages, and the other person will be grateful for your full engagement.

Pay attention to body language. Often, the person talking to you may say things like "I'm fine," but the person's body language—tight mouth, downturned lips, frowning, narrowed eyes, folded arms, body turned away from you—may offer clues to a different disposition. Body language is important, whether you are communicating with a spouse, a child, a boss, an employee, or a client. If you aren't focused on the person, you can miss important clues, and with them opportunities to be more successful in your communication.

Repeat back and check for understanding. This step is especially critical. Repeat what was said to you to find out whether you fully captured what the other person was trying to communicate. You can frame it in nonconfrontational ways, such as, "Just to make sure I understand, you're saying that . . ." Or, "I want to get this clear in my head: you feel that . . ." I can't overstate the importance of this step. When someone is speaking, we tend to filter the words and put them in our own context based on our personal backgrounds and paradigms. When I repeat back and check for understanding, most of the time I find that I've missed part of what was said. After I repeat to the speaker what I thought the message was, we worked together to make sure that I understood it completely.

"Deep listening is miraculous for both listener and speaker. When someone receives us with open-hearted, non-judging, intensely interested listening, our spirits expand."

—Sue Patton Thoele

Think about how important it is for you to fully understand the customer or client when a large sale is at stake! Just as important, imagine that you're trying to solve an issue with a spouse or a child, but you don't really understand what's causing the problem.

I try to be careful when using this method of repeating what someone has said. It needs to be done in a sincere manner so that the other person doesn't feel that I am being patronizing or just going through the motions of trying to understand. If it's sincere, it shouldn't feel like an interrogation.

In our seminars, we have people practice each of these steps, and it's especially fun to watch participants try this one. For some people, it is natural and comes easily. For others, it's a significant adjustment in the way they're used to communicating. Some people are accustomed to simply making their point heard as soon as the other person finishes speaking.

The importance of this particular step (repeating back to ensure that we understand) came to mind when a friend told us about visiting a local luxury car dealership. He went there intending to spend as much as $60,000 on a car. He was ready to buy, but the salesman he met was apparently not ready to listen.

Our friend told the salesman that he wanted a car with a leather interior and the latest technologies for such things as navigation systems and smartphone integration—all the bells and whistles. But instead of responding to that, the salesman went to a car, opened the hood, and started talking about the power and efficiency of its engine.

Our friend repeated that he was more interested in the comfort of the interior and the technologies, but the salesman insisted on telling him more about the engine. Our friend walked away from that salesman's dealership and took his $60,000 with him.

This story would have had a very different ending if the salesman had said, "Let me see if I understand what you're looking for. You want a car with a beautiful interior and all the latest bells and whistles, and that's what's most important to you. Is that correct?"

Then, once the salesman fully understood what our friend was looking for, he should have shown him a car with the desired features. Had the salesman done that, our friend would have written a check that day. Instead, the clueless salesman cost his company a considerable profit because he did not listen to a customer and respond to what that customer wanted.

I invite you to try this powerful step today with a partner, friend, or colleague. Try listening and then, when the person has finished speaking, politely repeating back and summarizing what you think the person said to ensure that you understood the full message.

Avoid Communication Roadblocks

While there are definitely steps you can take to improve your listening skills and your personal and professional communication, you should also be aware of certain obstacles to clear communication in the workplace and in your relationships. Some of these are related to tone, attitudes, and simple communication habits. Others may be the result of character flaws, prejudices, or insensitivities that need to be addressed if you hope to become your best and be a successful leader.

The late communications and conflict resolution expert Dr. Thomas Gordon identified 12 "roadblocks" to effective communication. I've adapted them with some adjustments for our purposes. Let's look at them and take measures to eliminate or overcome any of them that may be hindering your effectiveness as a communicator and leader.

- **Ordering, directing, and commanding.** Example: "You will do as you are ordered without question."

  Outside of the military, law enforcement, and dictatorships, the command and control model of communication tends to provoke resistance and resentment. Keep in mind that in most cases, leaders cannot be effective if they demand respect; they have to earn it and share it.

- **Warning, admonishing, and threatening.** Example: "If you miss that quota one more quarter, I'll find someone who can do the job."

  Most people do not respond well to threats or pressure. Some will do everything possible to resist and even rebel against this type of communication.

- **Moralizing, preaching, and imploring.** Example: "You, of all people, should have known better. I'm disappointed in you."

  Moral superiority is a tough mantle to wear well. No one likes to be treated like an inferior being. So, unless you've been granted the power of infallibility, you might follow the song lyrics that say, "Papa don't preach."

- **Advising or giving suggestions or solutions.** Example: "If it were me, I'd do it this way."

  This is one of those forms of communication that can be highly appropriate if you are training Eagle Scouts to rock-climb or instructing paratroopers on how to pack their chutes, but that may not be the best way to communicate with your department heads, your spouse, or the IT wizards you brought in to revamp your company software.

- **Persuading with logic, lecturing, or arguing.** Example: "If you are going to get the job done, you need to know what the heck you are doing."

  Lecturing is acceptable for college professors and drill sergeants, but the rest of us should try more listener-friendly approaches to persuasive communication. If you want those close to you and those who work with you to respond with enthusiasm, treat them as respected members of your team.

- **Judging, criticizing, and blaming.** Example: "How could you screw things up like this? What were you thinking?"

If you are awarding ribbons at the State Fair Hog
Competition, feel free to snort, grunt, poke, and be judg-
mental; otherwise, a more constructive and effective
approach would be to offer support, guidance, and encouragement rather than abuse.

- **Applying faint praise, left-handed compliments, and
buttering up.** Example: "Nice job, for a rookie."

    Praise, compliments, and encouragement are great com-
    munication tools when they are applied sincerely and in
    appropriate doses. If they are tainted with sarcasm or dipped
    in poison, they are more like knives in the back than like
    pats on the back.

- **Name-calling, ridiculing, and shaming.** Example: "That
was a really stupid move."

    Highly successful leaders treat those around them with
    respect and fairness. They don't rob them of their dignity or
    their self-confidence. If tearing people down becomes your
    default mode of communication, you are likely to bring
    yourself down, too.

- **Interpreting, analyzing, and diagnosing.** Example: "In
my opinion, you are screwing up because you aren't applying
yourself."

    This kind of communication is a block to listening
    because you are making assumptions and presumptions.
    Give others the opportunity to help you understand them
    and their actions before you form opinions about them and
    their performance.

- **Patronizing, false reassurance, and offering qualified
support.** Example: "Well, I guess it's not as bad as it could
have been."

    Those who work and live with you will be much more
    appreciative of honest, straightforward, and constructive
    communication than of words that simply don't ring true or
    are obviously insincere.

- **Probing, badgering, and interrogating.** Example: "Why weren't you in the office working on this proposal last night with the rest of your team? Did you have more important things to do?"

  If you are a homicide detective or a CIA interrogator, these forms of communication are acceptable. For the rest of us, it's best to remember that the most effective communication is conversational, not confrontational.

- **Distracting, diverting, and making light.** Example: "I know what you are going to say, and believe me, when this happened to me, I felt like a dummy, too."

  Making everything about you is a surefire way to shut down effective communication. Listen to understand and allow others to fully express their thoughts and feelings before you interpret their words through your own filters.

You will find that your success as an individual, and as a leader, will improve significantly if you remove these roadblocks to effective communication. Focus on being quick to listen and slow to wrath. If you do that, your comprehension will increase and your ability to communicate will improve. This is a breakthrough principle that helps you produce better results and improve your relationships. The results can be magical!

Master the Art of Feedback

Have you ever felt that you had a promising idea or suggestion, but there was no process for sharing it in your work, within an organization, or in a relationship? Or maybe you had an idea or suggestion, but you didn't feel comfortable sharing it.

Have you ever had problems in a relationship because you or another person let a problem or concern go too long without bringing it out into the open and discussing it to defuse the issue?

If you are a supervisor, when was the last time you asked one of your employees to offer suggestions on how you could be more effective as a leader? If you are an employee, when was the last time you asked your supervisor how you could improve your performance as an employee?

Feedback is free consulting! When we ask for and give feedback in the right way, it can make a tremendous difference in an organization or a relationship. In our research, we found that 30 percent of employees report frustration in their work because of poor communication—and a sense of frustration is one of the primary reasons that employees leave their jobs.

Let me share an example of the importance of feedback. We recently received a note from a talented individual who said that he'd become frustrated in his current job with one of the companies we trained. He'd been the company's top sales rep for three years in a row, but he didn't feel that he'd received any recognition for that accomplishment. He was considering leaving his job and finding work at a company where he could get more positive feedback for his efforts.

This is the perfect example of how critical it is to give and receive feedback in any organization or relationship. In this case, the company's top sales rep was ready to leave simply because he didn't feel that he was being recognized for his efforts. He was frustrated.

At any point along the way, this person's supervisors could have provided him with positive feedback that would have alleviated his frustration and made him feel valued. Or his supervisor could have asked him for feedback on how he could be a better leader or supervisor. By asking that simple question, the supervisor might have learned that this sales rep wanted recognition for his accomplishments.

The company eventually did respond, and the sales rep was grateful for the appreciation expressed. The company avoided the cost of losing a good employee, the cost of hiring another person, and the training costs that might have been incurred.

There's a wealth of information in feedback. Sometimes the reason that people don't ask for feedback is that they don't want a confrontation or they feel awkward doing so. There is a very practical method for gathering feedback in the form of ideas, suggestions, and concerns without creating conflict. This great tool can help open channels of communication in a business, with a partner, or even with a son or daughter. It involves a three-step process called Continue–Start–Stop. On Figure 7.1 or on a separate sheet of paper that copies the illustration, write your responses.

1. Below the word "*Continue*," write your ideas or suggestions for things that work well and that you would like the person or organization to continue doing.

2. Below the word "*Start*," write your ideas and suggestions for things you would like the person or organization to start doing that aren't currently being done.

1. Continue

2. Start

3. Stop

FIGURE 7.1 Continue–Start–Stop Tool

3. Below the word "*Stop*," write your suggestions for things
   that the person or organization should stop doing because,
   in your view, they are not working well.

You can use this three-step method to provide feedback to
others or to solicit feedback from others for yourself or your
organization. Although it takes some courage to invite others to
provide feedback like this, if the feedback is sincere, specific, and
constructive, it can be invaluable for improving communication
and helping relationships get to a better place.

We consistently use this feedback tool throughout our company. I've also used it with my wife and children, and they've
certainly given me some great feedback! There were things I was
doing personally that I never knew were bothering my family
members until I gave them a chance to provide feedback with the
Continue–Start–Stop tool. I invite you to try this with your family members or employees and see what they come up with.

In one of our seminars, we gave the Continue–Start–Stop
tool to a client's employees. As a result of the feedback, the managers created a weekly newsletter for their team of 40 people. The
positive impact was immediate, and communication improved
throughout the company. The tool helped employees become
more engaged and more willing to share ideas, which made their
division more effective, increased customer satisfaction, and
improved revenues. This division became one of the most successful in the company, and many of the ideas came from the
Continue–Start–Stop exercise. This is a fun and powerful tool
for soliciting feedback.

Rate This on a Scale of 1 to 10

Early in my marriage, a friend taught me an easy and useful
method for improving communication and giving feedback that
involved using a 1 to 10 rating scale. Here is how it works. One
person simply asks the other to rate his or her feelings about a certain issue on a scale of 1 to 10.

A "10" means that you are *really excited*!

A "1," on the other hand, means *no way*.

We use this method for things as simple as deciding what to do on a date night: "How much do you want to go to a movie?" If one person said, "Seven," and the other said, "One," then we might consider other options. If my wife ever rates her interest in something at a 6 or below, I take note and adjust accordingly.

Not long ago we had a family gathering, and about 10 of us were sitting around after a long and tiring day. We needed to get milk for the next morning. I volunteered to get it, but in trying to recruit someone to tag along, I said, "Okay, I want everyone to be honest; on a scale of 1 to 10, how interested are you in going to the store with me?"

Tommy was working on something, and he said, "I'm at a 4!"

Michaela said, "I'm at a 1."

Rob said, "I'm at a 3!"

Tonya and my wife said, "We are at a 0!"

Daniel and Heather each reported 4.

Anne was a 5.

Coleman, our son-in-law, came in at a very precise 5.94.

That provoked laughter, but then he had a change of heart and gave it a 7, so he tagged along with me. A few others joined in, and we actually had a great time at the grocery store because no one felt that he'd been dragged along. This is a fun and simple technique to use with family members or colleagues.

Learn to Control Your Emotions

We've looked at several methods and tools for improving your listening and communication skills at work and in your personal life. A final area that many people find challenging is controlling their emotions, particularly their anger, when communicating in stressful situations.

A well-known Bible passage, written more than 2,000 years ago, advises us to be swift to hear, slow to speak, and slow to wrath. As admirable as that advice may be, it's often difficult to put into practice, especially in tense situations. Still, wrath, which can be defined as anger, impatience, being opinionated or prejudiced, or even expressing rage, is a major barrier to effective communication. It is also very difficult to build trust and teamwork when your emotions are out of control. Let's discuss both the impact of wrath and some tips for maintaining control in heated moments.

The ability to monitor and control your feelings in your communications and your actions is an indicator of emotional intelligence. You can't always control the feelings that come over you, but you can—and should—control how you act and communicate if you want to have a positive impact in your work and your relationships.

Communicating when you are wrathful usually alienates those who you are trying to influence or reach. Rarely does anything good come of it. More often, it results in bitterness, retaliation, and rejection. Marriages can be destroyed, and relationships can be ruined. Expressing wrath is rarely an effective way to strengthen relationships or to get to a better place in life.

Think about situations in which you've lost your temper while communicating with an employee or someone close to you. Was it effective? Did you get the desired results? Were communications and relationships improved?

Think also about situations in which you've controlled your temper and communicated without highly charged emotions. Was this effective? Did you get the desired results? Were communications and relationships improved as a result?

Expressing anger rarely does any good, as reflected in this saying that someone once shared with me: "If you give a lecture when you are angry, it will likely be the best lecture you ever regret."

In most daily interactions, communicating without wrath or intimidation proves more effective over the long run. One of my favorite poets, Charles Penrose, wrote something on this topic after becoming angry because of a false accusation. He had loaned furniture from his home to his longtime church for many years. Later, when the church was well established and was able to buy its own furnishings, Penrose reclaimed some favorite items, only to have some uninformed members accuse him of stealing church property.

Penrose was deeply offended by these accusations, and he felt great anger and indignation at being judged so harshly. However, he controlled his anger and used it to drive his creativity, writing a poem titled "School Thy Feelings." This has become one of my favorite poems; let me share a part of it with you:

> School thy feelings; there is power
> In the cool, collected mind.
> Passion shatters reason's tower,
> Makes the clearest vision blind. . . .
> Wound not willfully another,
> Conquer haste with reason's might;
> School thy feelings, sister, brother;
> Train them in the path of right.
>
> —"School Thy Feelings," Charles W. Penrose

There is so much wisdom in those words.

Penrose used his anger to create a poem that has lasted long beyond his lifetime, which reminds me of a story about a prominent older gentleman who explained to a reporter the secret to his living a long life: "Early in our marriage, we determined that if we ever got in a quarrel, one of us would leave the house until the feelings calmed down. I attribute my longevity to the fact that I have breathed a lot of fresh air throughout my married life."

Anger Management as a Communication Tool
Stepping back and giving yourself time to regain control of your emotions is a proven method for improving your communication skills.

One of the greatest practices that will enable you to avoid wrath is mastering patience. Replacing wrath with patience and focusing on listening and understanding work wonders. Step back and give yourself some time to work out the best way to communicate. Few things need to be resolved immediately, especially in heated moments. Rather than responding with wrath, listen with patience. The minute you revert back to listening, you get to a better place.

The next time you feel hot blood rising with emotion, say to yourself: "Don't react. Listen and understand." Sometimes the best course of action is to remove yourself from the situation temporarily until you start to calm down. If necessary, step outside and take deep breaths for a couple of minutes.

You can always go home and kick a pillow or punch a punching bag!

Control your emotions and practice patience, one of the greatest virtues in the universe. You can be a patient person and still be a mover and a shaker. Nelson Mandela managed to be patient during a 27-year imprisonment, and he had quite an impact, didn't he? So can you—and you don't have to go to prison to do it.

> "The wise old owl lived in an oak
> The more he saw the less he spoke
> The less he spoke the more he heard
> Why can't we all be like that wise old bird?"
> —Edward H. Richards

Start Today—Be an Effective Communicator

I've covered several areas that can have a direct and immediate impact on your ability to become a more effective communicator. This will help you develop deeper and more rewarding personal and professional relationships. I invite you to try some of them this week. You will benefit greatly by working on the keys to becoming an effective communicator, asking for feedback from your employees or your supervisor, resolving to address any anger issues, and removing any roadblocks to effective communication.

Being quick to listen and slow to wrath is not easy, I know. It's much more difficult to reach understanding than simply to react emotionally. I think that fact inspired the late children's book author and illustrator Robert McCloskey to offer this brain-twister, "I know that you believe you understand what you think I said, but I'm not sure you realize that what you heard is not what I meant."

As you become a more effective communicator, you will notice that your working and your personal relationships improve, as does your efficiency at work and at home. Most highly successful leaders master the principle of being "quick to listen and slow to wrath." The practice of this principle inspires, strengthens, and encourages others. You, in turn, become more insightful, more productive, and more creative as an individual and a team member.

This inspiring behavior leads to greater effectiveness and success and to the best outcomes. Being an effective communicator is a total game changer that will consistently bring out your best and the best in your organization!

Leadership Action Steps

1. One of the greatest gifts you can give to others is to really listen to them and to be fully with them as they talk to you.

2. Be an effective communicator in your personal and professional life:

   - Look the person in the eyes.

   - Focus on the words, not on what you'll say next.

   - Pay attention to body language.

   - Acknowledge the person's feelings or questions

   - Repeat back and check for understanding.

3. Avoid the 12 roadblocks to effective communication.

4. Feedback is the breakfast of champions! Don't fear it; embrace it. Use the Continue–Start–Stop tool to solicit feedback from your employees, supervisors, spouse, and children.

5. Use the 1 to 10 rating scale method to assess family members' or coworkers' desire to engage in a particular activity.

6. Put a "check" on your wrath, instead seeking only to listen, understand, and fully capture the other person's point of view. Control your anger, opinions, pride, emotional baggage, tendency to take offense, and prejudice, and focus instead on true listening.

7. Remember the quote, "If you give a lecture when you're angry, it will probably be the best lecture you ever regret!"

8. When speaking to others, be clear and concise.

9. Be quick to listen and slow to wrath.

CHAPTER 8

Innovate Through Imagination

Think outside the box for success in business and life.

How would *you* explain the twenty-first century to a time traveler from medieval times? It's difficult knowing where to begin! Think about how far we've come, and now think of the possibilities that lie ahead!

- High-speed Internet
- Mind-controlled robotic limbs
- 3D printers
- Space tourism
- Electric cars
- Smartphones
- Medical miracles
- Wearable computers

From research into what makes individuals, companies, and organizations successful, we identified common success factors in the long-term highest achievers, and one of them was the ability to tap the power of imagination to innovate and remain relevant over many years and decades. It's about creating opportunities and possibilities in your personal and professional lives.

The human imagination is capable of producing endless opportunities and possibilities. With them comes *hope* and the belief that there are solutions to problems. There are ideas waiting to be acted upon. There are many options available! This is the spirit of innovation driven by the imagination. Imagine the effect it might have on your company if each of your employees felt empowered to constantly find innovative ways to serve your customers and clients and to make your product or service better. World-class companies have risen to the top of global business by tapping the imaginations of the best and the brightest. What about your business? How might it benefit from inspired and imaginative employees who are constantly striving to do things better, faster, and smarter?

In just about every company or industry, you can bet that there's someone out there right now who is trying out an innovative idea that could put your company out of business. If you're not on the leading edge of finding new and better ways to do what you do, then remember that potential competitors are looking for an opportunity to do just that.

I recently attended a gathering of world leaders from the World Presidents' Organization. One of the speakers brilliantly articulated some new disruptive technologies and how they would completely change the business landscape. He even suggested that as many as 40 percent of the current Fortune 500 companies could be rendered obsolete in the next 10 years because of disruptive technologies.

Four Secrets of Innovation

The Walt Disney Company has been one of the most successful corporations in the world for decades upon decades. Is it just coincidence that it has a department known as "Imagineering" with a team that includes 140 job titles, including illustrators, architects, engineers, lighting designers, writers, and graphic designers?

Tapping the power of the imagination has elevated Disney, Apple, Google, Tesla, SpaceX, and many other leading corporations to the top of their fields. They have failures. They make mistakes. But they are empowered to learn from those failures and mistakes and to focus on solutions rather than problems.

Ordinary people accomplish extraordinary things when they unleash their imaginations in the workplace and in their lives. We all have the gift of imagination.

True, some people are more creative than others, but we all have imaginations. It's not about your level of creativity as much as it's about whether you wield your creative powers as effectively as possible. Albert Einstein claimed that imagination is more important than knowledge. Imagination leads to discovery and innovation.

Ideas must be conceived in our minds before they can become a reality. Once an idea is developed, it starts growing and takes shape. However, you must first dare to use your imagination to get the ball rolling.

Every invention sprang from someone's imagination. Elon Musk imagined an electric car that was not a compromise, but an advance in technology, and he created Tesla. The innovative minds at Google imagined a wearable computer, and they produced Google Glass. J. K. Rowling, a struggling single mother, imagined the Harry Potter novels, which delighted and engaged millions of fans and transformed her own life as well.

These breakthroughs arose from the imaginations of regular men and women who were working to stay ahead of an ever-changing world. Can you recall a time when you imagined an outcome and then it happened?

Before starting any project, job, or new endeavor, first imagine your desired outcomes: What are the possibilities? What would be the greatest thing imaginable? Then get busy making it a reality.

I've made it a habit to ask myself every day: "Is my imagination switch in the 'on' position? Have I flipped the switch to my imagination?"

New possibilities, solutions, answers, and options are created when you turn on the switch to your imagination. They begin to flow like electric current through a lightbulb and power to a computer when their switches are turned on. The use of your imagination will bring hope, excitement, and confidence to you, your team, and your businesses!

First comes the idea, the inspiration, or the vision, and then comes the process for making your dream a reality. Imagination also allows us to sketch out the pathway to that reality. It creates the magic in our lives, our businesses, and our organizations.

So, how can you be sure your imagination switch is "on"? How do you turn it on and fire it up? I've identified four proven ways for firing up your imagination.

1. Be curious and ask the right questions.

2. Create a brainstorm of possibilities.

3. Walk away and let your subconscious do the work.

4. Write about your ideas.

Let's look at each of these ideas in more depth so that you can put them to practical use in your business, your organizations, and your everyday life.

Be Curious and Ask the Right Questions

Imagination can be turned on and fired up by curiosity. Take a look at one of the most significant inventions of our age: it can be argued that the core competency of the Wright Brothers was curiosity. They went beyond merely observing that flight was possible. They asked the key "Why?" and "Why not?" questions: "Why can birds fly? Why not man?" Is it possible that the invention of manned flight went to the team that was more curious, asked more questions, and practiced more persistently?

Curiosity is a pathway to imagination because it creates questions in the mind—and the mind wants answers to those questions. The process of seeking answers results in more questions. As you ask more and more questions, your mind becomes more focused, the quality of your questions improves, and solutions arise. Higher-quality questions result in higher-quality information. Einstein said, "The important thing is to not stop questioning. Curiosity has its own reason for existing. . . . I have no special talents. I am only passionately curious."

I love the quote from the children's book author Dr. Seuss: "Think left and think right and think low and think high. Oh, the thinks you can think up if only you try!" It takes a conscious effort to flip on the switch to our imagination.

The ability to ask questions cultivates curiosity. Continually asking *How? What? Where? When? Why? Who?* helps you see things with greater clarity. Let me share an example to illustrate this idea.

Great Innovators

Thomas Edison was born in 1847. He was an inventor, a scientist, and a businessman. Edison patented 1,300 inventions. Those inventions included the phonograph, the motion picture camera, and a long-lasting, practical electric lightbulb. He greatly influenced life around the world. The list of his inventions staggers the mind, and their impact is so vast that it is impossible to measure.

I recently attended a speech by a modern-day creative genius who is following in Edison's footsteps, Dr. Patrick Soon-Shiong, and I came away convinced that the imagination is an even more powerful force when it is paired with modern technologies. Born in 1952—one hundred years after Edison—Dr. Soon-Shiong is a surgeon, medical researcher, CEO, philanthropist, and professor at the University of California at Los Angeles. He is one of the preeminent scientific and medical minds in the world today.

Dr. Soon-Shiong has a great creative vision. He has pioneered treatments for diabetes and cancer, publishing more than 100 scientific papers and filing more than 95 U.S. patents. He performed the world's first encapsulated human islet transplant, which involves transplanting an isolated mass of tissue from a donor's pancreas into another person to stimulate the production of insulin as a treatment for type 1 diabetes.

This remarkable man also performed the first pig-to-man islet cell transplant in diabetic patients. In addition, he pioneered the use of Abraxane for the treatment of breast cancer, and this groundbreaking drug is now in trials for treating lung, gastric, and pancreatic cancer and melanoma. Dr. Soon-Shiong is an entrepreneur as well. He has developed and sold two multibillion-dollar pharmaceutical companies.

How could anyone accomplish so many things? Highly successful people fire up their imaginations with an insatiable desire to understand how things work. Their curiosity is boundless. Their lives and accomplishments are built upon creativity and drive as well as powerful intellects.

> "Around here, however, we don't look backwards for very long. We keep moving forward, opening up new doors and doing new things, because we're curious . . . and curiosity keeps leading us down new paths."
>
> —Walt Disney

Strive for Your Best Ideas

As you fire up your imagination, one of the most important questions that you can ask yourself is, "What does my best look like?"

As you ask and re-ask this question and apply it to many different situations in your life, a flood of different answers and ideas will come to mind. What you may find amazing is how the answers to this same question differ as you move through the stages of life. By the way, be sure to have a place to write things down as you ask yourself "best questions."

Once you've asked these questions, you have engaged your mind to seek answers. Here's an example from an organizational perspective: What does the best performance in your organization look like? How can the best performance be measured? What types of behavior are needed to accomplish this type of performance? What can you do to make a unique contribution within your organization? How do you maximize safety as an organization? How can people within your organization communicate better?

A great way to get your creative juices flowing is to open a notebook, or, as I call it, a thoughts book, and put pen to paper. The simple act of writing down your ideas can create a flood of thoughts. If you'd like to try this experiment, open your thoughts book and follow these steps:

- Choose an area of your life that needs improvement.

- Start asking questions about what your best looks like in that area. You might be able to use some of the questions I used in the previous examples.

- From your list of questions, choose one that, if answered appropriately, could really make a significant difference in your life right now. Write as many ideas as you can think of to answer that question. Do this exercise for a set period of time, say 5 to 10 minutes.

- Circle or star the "best" idea or ideas on your list.

- Write your response to this question: If this idea were implemented, what impact would it have on me, on others, or within our organization?

This is a powerful exercise that can help you find actionable ways to bring some of your newly found ideas into being.

So the first way to "flip the imagination switch" to the on position is to increase our curiosity and ask the right questions. Let's look at the next idea.

Create a Brainstorm of Possibilities

At business school, we opened our minds to fresh approaches by studying innovations from the past and then discussing them in our study groups. This was a remarkable process because each student added something to our understanding. I learned that having different perspectives is critical to innovation. That's what brainstorming involves: tapping the mental energies of a group in order to trigger every participant's imagination. Over and over, I've found that when you enlist the help of others, the number of new and fresh ideas goes up exponentially.

Brainstorming can be very powerful, both individually and as an organizational exercise. I've had the chance to consult with many companies around the world, and most of them simply didn't know how to organize a brainstorming session. In our seminars, we help teams brainstorm over a real opportunity or problem, and when they leave, they are always excited about going back and using this powerful tool with others.

Here are some thoughts and suggestions on how to brainstorm effectively. You can use them personally or within your company.

1. Form a brainstorming group (a council, forum, mastermind group, or any other form you'd like to create) with somewhere between two and eight participants. If there are more than eight members, it's almost too many to really capture ideas effectively.

2. Choose a leader for the brainstorming and start with the vision of what you hope to accomplish. Do you want to solve

a problem or challenge, to create a new opportunity, or to create a fresh idea or approach?

3. Do not engage in criticism. Support one another. This is designed to foster the free flow of ideas, no matter how radical they may be. Brainstorming is about quantity, not quality. If we criticize someone's idea, that person may stop contributing to the exercise.

4. Take 5 to 20 minutes. Sometimes, if the problem is complex, it may take a lot longer than 20 minutes, but usually that is enough time to flush out some great thoughts.

5. Have a scribe capture the ideas.

6. Once you're done and the ideas are on paper, narrow down the list to two or three of the most actionable ideas and see which ones are worthy of being explored and developed more fully.

> "Imagination is everything. It is the preview of life's coming attractions."
> —Albert Einstein

The Smell of Success

If you follow these simple steps, you can unlock a world of ideas for dealing with even the most complex problems. Let me give you a spicy real-world example of the power of brainstorming and how it transformed an entire brand.

Old Spice totally redefined itself in 2008 through a brilliant and fun marketing campaign. Prior to 2008, Old Spice was a struggling brand. It was commonly viewed as the scent preferred by elderly gentlemen. In 2008, the brand's owner, Procter & Gamble, recognized the problem. The company decided to flip the switch by creating more imaginative marketing.

It rebranded Old Spice, giving it a new, fresh look and attitude—a swagger—and targeting males in the 12–34 age bracket.

The new marketing campaign implied that Old Spice could transform nerdy wimps into manly dudes. The commercials were done with humor and flash, and they worked. The aging brand was revitalized, growing 400 percent in just one year!

How Brainstorming Saved a Company

Let me share with you a more personal example of how brainstorming helped save an entire company.

Crystal, a very capable and talented friend of mine, lost her father in a plane accident. He had been the president and primary owner of the Flying J truck stops. Within a short time, the CFO informed Crystal that the company was heading toward a severe cash shortage: about $300 to $400 million. He informed her that it looked as if the company was headed for bankruptcy.

This was a devastating blow for Crystal, her capable husband, Chuck, and the rest of the executive team. Most of her advisors told Crystal that there was no way to save the company. The company was at great risk, and the situation seemed absolutely overwhelming. Crystal did something that gave her hope and, in retrospect, probably saved the company. She called together the key stakeholders, plus some experts who had a great deal of experience in bankruptcies, and held a brainstorming session. During that session, they came up with a plan of attack that was later approved by the bankruptcy court and the company's creditors. Through hard work, determination, and grit, they implemented the plan and saved the company. In fact, it became more profitable than ever before.

Crystal credits the brainstorming session with saving the family business. Because of that gathering of minds, she overcame incredible, almost impossible odds. When everyone else was saying that there was no way, she and her brainstorm team put their imaginations to work and found a way. She found solutions when most people told her there were no solutions to be found.

Again, this is the power of actually sitting down with key people and brainstorming new ideas. This group changed the game for this business. You can do the same for yours. Create your own mastermind group. Challenge it to come up with creative solutions and innovations. Make it fun and exciting so that everyone feels fully engaged and appreciated. Be attentive to the surge of ideas and thoughts that results. You may have to repeat this process numerous times to ultimately get the result that you want, but it's almost always worth it.

The first two steps, then, in flipping on the imagination switch are:

1. Be curious and ask the right questions.

2. Create a brainstorm of possibilities.

Let's look at the third idea.

Walk Away and Let Your Subconscious Do the Work

Thomas Edison frequently let his subconscious do the innovative work for him. While struggling to create the electric lightbulb, he and his team made slow progress. They finally created filaments that would last more than 40 hours, but those filaments were too expensive. Edison's team went back to work, spending many more hours focused on the problem.

The team came up with nothing workable during those intense work sessions. But Edison traveled to observe a total eclipse of the sun on July 29, 1878, from the Continental Divide.

While Edison was relaxing on that trip, his mind came up with an innovative solution to the lightbulb problem. One day, while fishing, Edison realized that the bamboo in his fishing pole had certain properties that they'd been looking for to create a longer-lasting lightbulb filament. In the end, his little fishing break produced a carbonized bamboo filament that allowed a lightbulb to burn 1,200 hours rather than 40 hours.

Edison thought he'd left the problem of the filament back at his lab in New Jersey, but in his relaxed state, his subconscious mind devised a solution.

Awaken Your Imagination Through Sleep

How many times have you come out of a deep sleep with a solution to a problem of your own? Use that power. Relax for success! If you're afraid to take a break because it'll make you feel like a slacker, call it an "incubation period" instead of a vacation. *Incubation* is defined as a time when a problem is "parked" in your subconscious. You can't see any progress being made, but your mind is quietly whirling away. Many of my most successful ideas have come when I stepped away and went for a walk outside. Sometimes the subconscious can unlock amazing ideas when we least expect them, so we should be open and ready for them. When the ideas do come, make sure you write them down and capture them.

Sometimes the simple act of stepping away from the problem will free your mind and unleash your imagination.

The final way for unlocking your imagination is a very simple, but effective one.

Do It Like da Vinci—Keep a Thoughts Book

It's no accident that the word *write* follows the other three steps we've talked about. Writing can be a rich and vital part of boosting your imagination. There is power in writing, as I mentioned earlier; often the simple act of putting pen to paper will allow your thoughts to flow. Leonardo da Vinci's thoughts books—notebooks in which he recorded thoughts, sketches, concepts, and images—provide insights into his methods for firing his incredible imagination and creativity. Some see him as the quintessential engineer, a person who was able to effectively combine scientific intellect with artistic creativity. Da Vinci was a master at capturing ideas in his notebook, and they serve as powerful examples of this method for igniting your imagination. I've found that highly successful leaders will often write their ideas and thoughts. Figure 8.1 shows just a couple of examples from da Vinci.

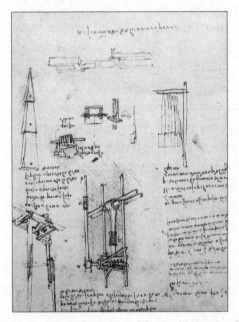

FIGURE 8.1   A Page from One of da Vinci's Notebooks

Let's look at a more modern and down-to-earth example. John Reed was a senior vice president at Citibank who later served as its chief executive and then became president of the New York Stock Exchange. While relaxing on vacation early in his career, he jotted down some notes as ideas came to him. Those recorded thoughts would change not only his business, but also the entire industry.

He wrote 30 pages of ideas. As these ideas began to take shape, they became a blueprint for a new kind of bank—one that offered the national marketing of credit cards and street-level cash machines. This led to the birth of the ATM.

John Reed, Albert Einstein, Leonardo da Vinci, Anne Frank, Winston Churchill, Maya Angelou, Ralph Waldo Emerson, Marie Curie, and Orville and Wilbur Wright lived at different times and in different places, but they had one thing in common: they understood how important capturing their thoughts on paper could be. Many of the most successful people I've met are avid note takers and journal keepers. They record their thoughts and ideas to capture them for future action. There is something very magical about simply putting a pen to paper, or your finger to a keyboard, when it comes to translating thoughts into actions.

Sometimes your imagination can be freed only by writing. In fact, simply picking up a pen and paper or your notepad can unleash your inner genius. There is freedom in just letting your thoughts flow without criticism or judgment. Writing can help you clarify and organize ideas that might otherwise slip away.

Writing has significance and power because it combines the mind and the body, resulting in a focus that is not possible with other kinds of thinking. Writing in your notebook or digital device can create feelings of both peace and progress—peace as you write about the pressures of family or work life, and progress as you record your goals and make notes of your dreams for your life. Once you've written down your vision, it is hard to erase.

Writing can be lonely and time-consuming. The Oscar-winning screenwriter Michael Kanin said, "I don't like to write, but I love to have written." You're not trying to be a writer; you're trying to be a recorder of your inner and outer world. Your thoughts and ideas are a revelation from your inner mind to your conscious self. Those thoughts are important. You're having them pretty much all the time, and you need to give them air by recording them.

The act of writing opens up entire new vistas, views, and majestic scenery. Harriet Beecher Stowe thought *Uncle Tom's Cabin* was written through her by "another hand." The point is that writing connects you to your inner mind, which in turn is connected to a higher mind or higher source of inspiration.

Putting words on paper opens up the creative mind to fresh approaches and perspectives. Nobel Prize winner Albert

Szent-Györgyi, who discovered vitamin C, said, "Look at the same thing as everyone else and think something different." It is in these moments of creative illumination that answers to personal, relationship, and organizational problems are revealed.

Some of the most successful people in history captured their thoughts in writing. If you don't already have a notebook, I encourage you to go out and invest in a thoughts book. This can be as simple as a spiral notebook from an office supply store or taking notes on your digital device. I invite you to keep these tools near you and make a purposeful effort to capture ideas and thoughts when they come. I also invite you to make time at least once a week to capture recent events or ideas.

Imagineer Your Business and Your Life

This guiding constant is all about feeling free to flip on the switch to your imagination. We've looked at four ways to do that:

1. Be curious and ask the right questions.

2. Create a brainstorm of possibilities.

3. Walk away and let your subconscious do the work.

4. Write about your ideas.

Your imagination is one of the greatest gifts that you possess. Author John Steinbeck shared, "Ideas are like rabbits. You get a couple and learn how to handle them, and pretty soon you have a dozen."

Whether you are a sales representative trying to figure out how to increase sales or a division manager working to expand revenues and improve margins, don't be afraid to tap into your creativity.

If you are a parent or grandparent trying to guide your family through challenges, tap into your imagination to inspire them.

Whether you are trying to solve a tough problem or simply seeking to be your best, you have inner resources for finding solutions and motivation.

Start today! Ignite and fire up your imagination.

Progress begins with and depends upon the use of your imagination. When you turn on the switch to your imagination, you open the door to the possibility of your *best* new ideas. Imagine this: your best is yet to come!

Leadership Action Steps

1. Stoke your curiosity. Ask questions. For example, *What does my best look like?* In a relationship, you could ask, *What does our best look like?* For a company, you might ask, *What does our best as an organization look like?*

2. Use questions that help to produce answers. Ask *Who? What? Why? Where? When? How?* Is the potential solution ethical and in line with your character?

3. Be sure that the switch to your imagination is "flipped on." Think and dream of possibilities.

4. Collaborate and brainstorm—consider all options. Everything is fair game. Invite others to join in the imaginative process.

5. Walk away—let your subconscious mind do its work.

6. Get a fresh sheet of paper and a pen. Think of your problem or opportunity. What is the hoped for outcome, the vision? Now list as many ways as you can think of to get closer to that vision and outcome. Write, write, write! Set the sheet aside. Then revisit it and write some additional thoughts and ideas.

PART THREE

Transformational Living

**12 Principles of
Highly Successful Leaders**

12 Never Give Up!

1 Be True to Character

11 Live in Peace and Balance

2 Lead with a Vision

LIVING

LEADERSHIP

10 Apply the Power of Knowledge

TRANSFORMATIONAL

3 Manage with a Plan

9 Be Accountable

4 Prioritize Your Time

TEAMS AND RELATIONSHIPS

8 Innovate Through Imagination

5 Live the Golden Rule in Business and in Life

7 Be an Effective Communicator

6 Build and Maintain Trust

CHAPTER 9

Be Accountable

Take responsibility and do what you say you will do.

One day not long ago, I got up early, made some toast with jam, grabbed a quick glass of orange juice, and headed out to exercise. When I returned, my wife, Roxanne, had gone out on some errands, and the note you see in Figure 9.1 was taped to the toaster.

This was my opportunity to make a choice. I could take responsibility, or I could blame the problem on something else— the toast, my being in a hurry, my mother, or just being a man. What would you do?

Fortunately, I made a wise decision and accepted responsibility. I cleaned up the mess, leaving a smooth, clean countertop and making sure that no crumbs fell on the floor. Then, I left the note you see in Figure 9.2 in place of Roxanne's note and went to work in my office, which is near the kitchen.

When Roxanne returned home, I listened carefully; when I heard her laughing, I knew that she had read my note. I was grateful that she had written such a positive, upbeat note to offer feedback and help me see a better way. I was also grateful that I

After making toast or whatever, please wipe the crumbs up with a wet cloth.

The <u>test</u> is to wipe your hand across the counter, and if the crumbs are all gone, yippee! It's clean!

P.S. And <u>PLEASE</u> don't wipe the crumbs onto the floor. THANK YOU !!!

FIGURE 9.1

Thank you for the feedback and training.

Well done. Nice smooth "crumbless" counters.

☺

FIGURE 9.2

had chosen to take responsibility rather than getting upset and angry. I will never leave crumbs on the counter or the floor again, if I can help it!

Fess Up and Own the Problem

We all fall short of expectations and make mistakes occasionally. An important part of being accountable is admitting that you have messed up and taking your medicine. You may be surprised at the reaction you get when you take responsibility rather than blaming something or someone. When there is a misunderstanding, confusion, a missed meeting, something that is not going right, or a mistake, simply fess up—take responsibility— and move on. When it's all over, take stock of what went right and what went wrong. Evaluate what you could have done better, jot down your thoughts, and then put the problem behind you. Go to bed, get some rest, and get ready for a fresh day tomorrow.

I've certainly made mistakes and missed opportunities to take responsibility. However, there was one situation I remember in my life where things could have gone badly but didn't because I took a chance and just fessed up. I was taking four people to the airport, and I almost missed the turnoff. We were talking, and I was distracted until it was almost too late to make the exit. I crossed several lanes of traffic and hit the exit just in time.

It would have ended there except for the highway patrolman who was right behind me. He was not amused by my fancy maneuver. On came his patrol car lights. I pulled over my car sheepishly. When the patrolman walked up to the window, I asked, "Is there a problem, officer?" (Quick to listen!)

"Sir, you crossed over three lanes to exit the highway," he noted.

He was right. I was wrong.

Normally I would have pleaded my case and explained my problem. This time, I decided that it was better to get this over with quickly so that my colleagues could get on their flight. I confessed and thanked him for pointing out my mistake. I took it on the chin and quickly admitted that I had made a mistake. I took full responsibility.

The officer asked for my insurance card, license, and registration. I thought I was sunk. He took my documents to his car and came back within a few minutes. He handed back my documents, and said, "Mr. Shallenberger, please be more careful and have a nice day!"

With that, he returned to his car, and I was able to get my colleagues to their gate. Score one for accountability!

In this case, taking responsibility for my actions had an immediate positive response. Rather than blaming someone or something or making an excuse, I admitted my mistake and accepted responsibility. I've been more careful about my driving ever since. In your business dealings or in your personal life, your particular situation may not involve crumbs on the counter or admitting to a police officer that you made a mistake, but it's the principle that counts.

There is an important distinction between "it's not finished" and "I haven't finished it." The difference is in your willingness to be accountable—to fess up—for what you do and what you fail or refuse to do. A willingness to fess up is a sign of character that signals to others that you keep your commitments.

People who aren't accountable tend to blame others or deny that they were responsible. Some even engage in psychological games, such as acting helpless and incapable of completing the task. Others may say that they were not aware of what was required or that other people did not step up. None of these behaviors takes you any closer to the victory. Fessing up does and taking responsibility does.

You may be tempted to offer one of the classic copouts: "I didn't know," "I wasn't there," "I didn't have time," or "It's not my job." But using those excuses creates more anxiety and doesn't take you toward personal or institutional success. Fess up and free yourself to become your best.

This principle, taking responsibility for your actions and their outcomes, can be one of the most liberating and energizing guiding constants. When we are accountable for our actions, significant improvement can begin to take place. The opposite of being accountable and taking responsibility is to place blame, criticize, complain, and condemn, which ultimately results in wasted time and energy.

Being accountable goes beyond just taking responsibility for your actions. One of the greatest roadblocks to personal success arises when a person blames or is constantly pointing fingers at others. Politicians are known for playing the blame game. They are constantly blaming their political opponents for everything that is wrong with the economy, world affairs, and even the weather.

It's much easier to move forward with your life and your business or career once you accept responsibility for your own situation instead of wasting time blaming circumstances or other people. Even when there's a reason to blame someone else or there's merit to your blame, taking responsibility for your life and actions gives you a starting point for moving forward.

One might argue that society is moving further and further away from personal accountability, given the blame game epidemic. Yet so many of your challenges could be fixed if you became more accountable and took responsibility for your actions and your circumstances.

If you're a business leader or manager, imagine the impact it would have if there were a culture of accountability within your team or business. Imagine the impact on the morale of your organization if people simply stepped up and took responsibility, rather than blaming others or their surroundings. This powerful chapter is all about creating a culture of accountability and taking personal responsibility for our actions.

To Act or Not to Act

Being accountable requires a determination to never give up.

To act or not to act? That is the question. Embedded in the commitment to be accountable is a commitment to do what you need to do to take control of your life and to become your best. You can't give up when the going gets tough, when being accountable is inconvenient, or when something else seems like more fun. I encourage you to commit to your core to achieve your best, no matter what. As Yoda from *Star Wars* so sagely put it, "Try not. Do . . . or do not. There is no try."

Can anyone give up after making a commitment to never give up? Sure; it happens all the time. But if it stops happening for you today—if you resolve right now to hold yourself accountable for your own success and happiness—you are taking a big step forward toward becoming your best.

There are few thrills like the thrill of victory over yourself. You can almost feel the excitement as you contemplate making that kind of commitment. When there is accountability, trust is higher. When there is accountability, people tend to do business with you.

Have you ever talked with a customer service rep who refused to accept responsibility and essentially blamed *you*, the customer? How did that make you feel? Did you want to continue doing business with that company? Of course not. How about the person who's constantly blaming others? How does that sound to you and how does it make you feel when you hear it? That's not who you want to be. You want to be someone who can be trusted, someone whom people enjoy being around. You want to be accountable.

Accountable Organizations: Fighter Pilot Culture of the Debrief

Is there a culture of responsibility and accountability within your organization and between you and your customers? Accountable organizations have accountable leaders. To be an accountable leader requires transparency, which builds trust.

I've shared a few stories about my sons who served in the U.S. Air Force. There are some great lessons to be learned from their experiences as fighter pilots. I've often described the fighter pilot culture as an excellent example of "trust building transparency." This same discipline exists in the other branches of the military as well.

As flight leaders, or "leads," the first thing Rob or Steven would do in the debrief (postflight review) after a mission was admit to any mistakes they might have made and describe what they could have done better.

The flight leads are transparent in their descriptions. In the debrief, they disclose everything to the other members of the flight before they give their notes and remarks. In their world, accountability begins with the flight leads. The flight lead uses "I" statements, not "we." The flight lead accepts ultimate responsibility by using the word *I*.

That's why a debrief is sacred to fighter pilots. They call it a "rankless" debrief. Generally there is a strict hierarchy in the U.S. Air Force, but in a rankless debrief, the leader opens up to those in the flight as though they were all on an equal standing. In the debrief, the focus is on *what's* right, not *who's* right. They set aside rank to get to the real issues. It's taking responsibility and using the word *I* that shifts the conversation to an atmosphere of open communication and accountability for their individual actions.

Isn't it true that you are often more open-minded when you hear your leaders speak candidly about their own performances and the improvements that they need to make?

As a leader, the next time you're going to critique or admonish an employee, first ask yourself whether there is anything that you, as the leader, could have done better. Did you, as the leader, ensure that the vision was clear? Did you provide clear directions and expectations? When you talk with your employees, you may find that if you start the discussion by focusing on what you could have done better, they will be much more open to your suggestions concerning what they could have improved. Accountable leaders and organizations take responsibility for all their actions.

Accountability Strategies

I want to share with you strategies and tools that can help you understand how to live with accountability as an individual and as a leader.

1. **Control what you can control.** Focusing your energy on what you can control empowers you to move away from criticism, complaints, and condemnations and forge ahead to become your best and achieve the highest levels of success.

2. **Develop relationship agreements.** These documents clearly define the vision, the reward system, the expectations, and the accountability in any relationship, personal or professional.

3. **Eliminate procrastination and follow through.** There are specific actions that you can take to improve your accountability.

Control What You Can Control

You can't control the terrible weather, bad drivers on the highway, incompetent restaurant chefs, irrational politicians, or that huge nail on the street that is about to put a hole in your $150 car tire.

You *can* control how you respond to all of these things, and that gives you much more power than you might ever have thought you had. In fact, by controlling your response to challenges, frustrations, and aggravations, you can greatly enhance the quality of your life.

One of the most effective things you can do to be accountable is to focus on the things that you can control rather than on the things that you cannot control. When you focus on what you can't control, the result is *wasted time and energy*.

You can't control others and you can't control a number of things around you, but you can control your actions, thoughts, and responses.

Let me illustrate this idea with a few examples of excuses offered by people who failed to complete projects by the deadline. This is the language of irresponsibility and blaming because they are not focused on controlling what they can control.

"It's their fault."

"I didn't have enough time."

"I couldn't get it done because they didn't give me enough information."

"The reason I failed is that my parents didn't teach me how to do it correctly."

This is the language of those who are focused on what they can't control. This kind of language lowers trust. Nobody really wants to be around it. When the going gets tough, it feels natural to complain and feel resentful not only about other people, but also about situations.

The implication is always: *This should not be happening to me. I don't want to be here. I don't want to be doing this. I'm being treated unfairly.*

On the other hand, someone who does focus on the things he can control might answer, "I accept full responsibility for that project," or, "I'm sorry this is late. I'll get the information and have it all delivered within two hours." Notice that there is no hint of blame or criticism in these two comments.

Those with accountable attitudes can focus their thoughts and actions on finding solutions instead of laying blame.

When I was 20 years old, I read a powerful passage from Dale Carnegie's *How to Win Friends and Influence People* that I've never forgotten:

"Any fool can criticize, condemn and complain—
and most fools do. But it takes character
and self-control to be understanding."

Complaining is not to be confused with informing someone of a mistake or deficiency so that it can be made right. Refraining from complaining doesn't necessarily mean putting up with bad quality or bad behavior. There's no problem with telling the waiter that your soup is cold and needs to be heated up if you stick to the facts, which are always neutral. However, if you say, "How dare you serve me cold soup," that's complaining.

Today and throughout your work, I invite you to monitor your thoughts to free yourself of complaints and blaming because both are usually the result of focusing on things that you cannot control instead of those that you can control. When you monitor your thoughts like that, you take control and change your focus to being proactive rather than reactive.

The Become Your Best 21-Day Challenge

In our seminars, we make a powerful invitation that has changed the lives of some participants. I invite you to try it, too: for the next 21 days, I invite you to focus only on *what you can control*. Take total ownership of your thoughts, words, and actions. That means that there are no excuses and no casting blame—only accepting responsibility. Scientists believe that it takes approximately 21 to 28 days to form a new habit, so try to make it through all three weeks! If you slip up, start over.

When one of our facilitators made this invitation in a corporate seminar, the CEO jumped out of his chair and shouted, "Yes!" I got a good laugh when I heard about that experience, and

I applauded the CEO for his willingness to try it with his entire company.

The entrepreneur and speaker Jim Rohn said it well, "You must take personal responsibility. You cannot change the circumstances, the seasons, or the wind, but you can change yourself. That is something you have charge of." Give yourself an opportunity to feel the thrill of victory over yourself. Feel the excitement as you make the commitment to focus only on what you can control. You can feel the liberating and energizing power of being accountable as you take responsibility for a positive outcome.

Develop Relationship Agreements

As you commit to becoming an accountable individual, you can lead your organization with greater responsibility, clarity, and ultimately success. No matter where you are, what's important is that you focus on your sphere of influence, and that will carry over to others.

In my experience as a leader of several organizations, I've used a transformative document called a *relationship agreement* that will increase accountability in your organization and your team. It will also increase your overall happiness, and probably the happiness of those who work with you and live with you. One of the primary reasons for workplace frustration is that employees don't understand their responsibilities or what is expected of them. This can lead to frustration from the perspective of both the supervisor and the employee. Setting clear expectations can lead to increased accountability and a clear understanding of what is to be accomplished. This can be done with employees, customers, and even your children.

What's nice about this is that it's something that you can control. I use the term *relationship agreement* to describe this document, which can help prevent miscommunication and misunderstandings. I used this with my sons when they were teenagers whenever I had a project for them to do. We also use it with our employees in our businesses today. Having a written relationship agreement helps avoid misunderstandings and sets clear expectations for both parties. If there are conflicts, it's easy to refer to the agreement.

The feedback from others is that this has been a remarkable tool in their organizations because of the way it helps both parties eliminate confusion. Relationship agreements are sometimes referred to as psychological contracts or win-win agreements. Let's take a look at the four elements that make up a relationship agreement.

1. What is the vision? The vision clearly describes the desired outcome. This puts everyone on the same page and inspires motivation.

2. What are the reward systems? When you specifically spell out the type of compensation, satisfaction, or any other type of incentive that employees will receive, you show them what's being done for them.

3. What are the expectations and guidelines? In this section, you clearly describe what is expected and the guidelines or standards. This is also the section where any key dates would be outlined, along with what's expected on those dates. This is also the place to describe any "watch outs" or "no-nos" from the perspective of the supervisor or the organization. This section ensures that the employee clearly understands what you are looking for and how to be effective in the organization.

4. How is accountability established? This is a great place to decide when progress on goals and other important milestones or projects will be reported. Take time to clearly describe the accountability process and how it works. Each organization may have a slightly different approach.

Take a moment right now to think of someone you know who could benefit from a relationship agreement with you, whether it's your child, an employee, or a service provider.

Try creating a relationship agreement by asking the four questions together:

1. What is the vision?

2. What are the reward systems?

3. What are the expectations and guidelines?

4. How is accountability established?

This is a powerful tool, and I encourage you to consider using it with your teams and your direct reports. If you have children and they're doing a job around the house, try using a relationship agreement. This can be a highly valuable tool for any leader.

We've used this for years in our various companies, and I've heard great feedback from both employees and supervisors. It has reduced workplace frustration for all involved and increased productivity because of the accountability and clear expectations that are built into the agreement.

Eliminate Procrastination and Follow Through

Relationship agreements take some thought up front, but they can save a significant amount of time and energy on the back-end. We've now gone through the first two tips: control what you can control and create relationship agreements. Now I want to share a few specific actionable strategies to help you increase personal accountability in every way. They are:

- Eliminate procrastination.

- Follow through.

Eliminate Procrastination: Do It! Do It Right!
Do It Right Now!

A friend of mine said his son's motto is, "Why do today what you can do tomorrow?"

He has to remind his son often that tomorrow never comes. But saying, "I'll do that tomorrow," can't be that bad, can it?

Yes, it actually can. Procrastination can become a debilitating habit, and it must be avoided—today! We are all tempted to procrastinate from time to time, thinking, "I'll get it done later."

If you do get the task done soon, that's fine, but for some people, putting things off becomes a default behavior, and it can become a serious problem. Procrastination is a breach of a commitment to act—a breach of trust. At the high end, procrastination could have a truly damaging effect.

How many people put off doing their taxes, paying their monthly bills, or renewing their driver's license, only to face greater difficulties as a result? Abraham Lincoln had it right: "You cannot escape the responsibility of tomorrow by evading it today."

So what do you do when the procrastination troll whispers in your ear: "It can wait"?

Lee Iacocca had a great answer: "Anything. Something. So long as we don't just sit there. If we screw up, start over. Try something else. If we wait until we've satisfied all the uncertainties, it may be too late."

Is anyone perfect at avoiding procrastination? I was going to provide an answer for that, but I decided to wait until later!

Okay, we are all prone to procrastinate now and then. Some of the most common causes of procrastination, though, can be managed. Distractions are the doors for procrastination, so do your best to eliminate them. This includes shutting down the e-mail and the Internet if you can't keep your hands off them when you are supposed to be doing other things.

Follow Through

Another key to mastering accountability is to follow through.

Recently I was at lunch with a friend, Jill, who told me how she had risen to become president of a very successful bank. She graduated with a degree in broadcast journalism, but when that career path did not pan out, she decided to work for a local bank. She remained there for 13 years, steadily rising to a significant leadership position. When a larger banking corporation purchased her institution, she became president of the entire organization.

Jill was promoted many times in the course of her career, and she earned the top position because of her ability to follow through and deliver on things that she said she would do. Her supervisors always knew that Jill was reliable. She also set personal goals over the years, including pursuing and obtaining an executive MBA.

Jill worked hard to balance her personal, family, and professional life so that she was highly successful in all three areas. In fact, Jill told me that she flew to Chicago to interview for the president's position just two weeks after she had her third child. She made sure that her baby was in good hands with family members before leaving town, of course. Jill did have some doubts that the company would give her the job, but she had established her reputation for diligence, commitment, and accountability.

This type of "be responsible" ethic has made all the difference in her life and her career. Jill serves as a role model to many people who aspire to be leaders in business and organizations. I think that's great. Following through on commitments and being accountable are important attributes in anyone who is pursuing a career or dedicated to a cause.

Do what you say you will do and do it in a timely manner, and you too will rise in your chosen field. If there is a problem or a good reason to withdraw your commitment, make sure you communicate with the people involved so that they can make adjustments if necessary.

Here are a few things that can help you follow through:

- Write down, in your organizer or calendar, what you have committed to do right away, so that you don't forget to do it. You can immediately start working, mentally and physically, to fulfill your commitment. Avoid writing things on scraps of paper. Those will get lost, and you will soon be swamped by little pieces of paper.

- Set yourself up for success. Organize your response in advance. Make a phone call list. Create a folder for materials that will help you get the job done.

- Get other people involved if necessary so that you don't get caught in a logjam. Give others as much advance notice as possible if you need their help so that you avoid creating problems for them. Don't procrastinate. Do it now! Action! Go! Step it up!

- Make follow-through part of your vision by using affirmations: "I follow through on my commitments." "People can count on me." "I am dependable." This type of affirmation of personal core values will work wonders.

- Do pre-week planning (discussed in Chapter 4). This will help you to stay ahead of the game and do your follow-through work on the things that matter most.

The Possibilities of Just One Person

When just one individual commits to eliminating procrastination and following through, that person can make an astounding difference. Reverend Will Bowen of Christ Church Unity in Kansas City, Missouri, has a vision of ridding the world of complaining. His attention to accountability exemplifies the enormous possibilities of one committed individual.

"The one thing we can agree on," said Reverend Bowen, "is that there's too much complaining."

This minister challenged his congregation to refrain from complaining, criticizing, using sarcasm, or gossiping for 21 days. That's three weeks! This is the same challenge that I issued earlier in the chapter. Everyone who pledged to accept the challenge was given a purple bracelet embossed with "Complaint Free World." Anyone who slipped up had to change the bracelet to the other wrist and start counting the days all over again.

It took the minister himself three and a half months to achieve 21 consecutive complaint-free days. Some members of his congregation took as long as seven months to reach the goal. It's obviously not easy, but it's an idea that has resonated with millions since that humble beginning in Kansas City, Missouri. As of this writing, the organization's website reports having distributed more than 9.8 million bracelets. If the average person complains 20 times a day for 30 days, then 9 million bracelets have stopped almost 5.5 billion complaints this month alone! Now that's nothing to complain about.

The obvious benefit of the 21-day challenge is that it helps end the habit of complaining. The less obvious but even greater benefit is that the noncomplainers save time and energy while focusing on more positive things. The time spent complaining may even be spent on achieving great things.

Be Accountable

In taking a final accounting, I've written a bit about focusing on those things that are under your control rather than complaining about those that are not. That also means that you don't complain about or criticize others. As Maya Angelou said, "If you don't like something, change it; if you can't change it, change your attitude. Don't complain."

The second step to improve accountability that I offered was a tool called a relationship agreement. These agreements will help give you greater clarity and unity in your organization's vision.

Each person in the relationship will understand the vision, what the rewards will be, what is expected, and exactly how to meet those expectations.

I encourage you to be accountable in every way. This means eliminating procrastination and following through with what you say you will do.

I've seen people who have embraced accountability transform their lives. I've had people tell me that this shift in attitude allowed them to let go of something they've been holding onto for years! Once they've figured out a way to let go and accept responsibility, most people feel free and empowered to move on with their lives. I've also seen increased accountability transform the culture of organizations. When employees take responsibility and refuse to blame others, great strides can be made.

You may have already noticed that the title of this principle includes the word *be*. This refers to a state of being, an inner state of the self that is immovable and ever present.

To be accountable is not only to "do" something—it is to "be" something, to be whole and balanced. It is to acquire, fully develop, and live the principles in a deep and meaningful way.

Virtually every successful example of accomplishment or achievement thoughout the history of the world, whether in a personal or a professional setting, is accompanied by alignment with the principles behind the guiding constants. On the flip side, virtually every failure results from a violation of the constants.

Creating an environment in which your thoughts can regularly be focused on these principles allows the principles to influence your actions, which ultimately allows them to be a powerful force of habit in your everyday life. These habits then contribute to your being a strong individual, having strong relationships, and exercising strong leadership and management for good.

Let the guiding constants act as a blueprint for you. Cultivate them, and they will be a mighty force in your life and the lives of many others.

Leadership Action Steps

1. Determine today to take responsibility for your actions, circumstances, and feelings. Resolve that you will focus only on your actions, rather than blaming, whining, or criticizing.

2. When describing your performance, use "I" instead of "we" to create a climate of open communication. People are more likely to listen to a leader who first takes responsibility.

3. Control what you can control. You waste your time and energy when you spend them on things that are outside of your control. Real transformation begins when you focus on what you *can* control.

4. Accountability cannot exist without proper accounting practices; an absence of accounting means an absence of accountability.

5. Create a relationship agreement. Clearly define the vision, reward systems, expectations, and guidelines, and determine how accountability is established.

6. Eliminate procrastination. Do it. Do it right. Do it right now!

7. Try the 21-day challenge: go for 21 days without blaming or criticizing others.

8. Create a learning circle to increase your accountability. Find someone you trust with whom you can share your goals and dreams. Simply sharing your goals makes the probability of success go up by 33 percent.

9. Your success or failure depends on you.

CHAPTER 10

Apply the Power of Knowledge

Learn, learn, learn, and apply what you've learned to reach new heights.

I was a happy child, but my childhood home was neither affluent nor peaceful. My parents divorced. My father remarried, and I lived first with my mom and then with my dad until I could move out, which I did several months before my eighteenth birthday. I'd always worked at a couple of jobs, so I knew that I could find a way to pay my rent. My first apartment was in a Vallejo neighborhood where people sometimes disappeared. Some of them turned up dead, including a guy who lived a block from me. Eventually, the police figured out that he was one of the victims of the infamous—and never captured—Zodiac Killer.

I slept with one eye open for the first few months, but after that, I grew too tired to worry. My main job was cleaning up rental properties owned by one of my early mentors and role models, Dave Conger, an entrepreneur with many holdings who took me under his wing. I also worked on a garbage truck for the city whenever I could get hired as one of the shift laborers. It paid

$16 an hour (serious money for me), but I had to stand in line at 4:30 a.m. and hope to be called to duty. As you might imagine, it was not pleasant work, but it was more enlightening than you might suspect.

The city gave you a huge garbage can that was capable of holding three residential garbage cans. I had to flip it on my shoulder and go from yard to yard, picking up garbage and tossing it in the truck hopper. Vallejo was a hardscrabble blue-collar town, and my parents had been scraping by, so I wasn't a spoiled kid. Still, my coworkers on the garbage truck were generally immigrants, and they were poorer and tougher than any people I'd ever known. They weren't working to pay for new cars and color televisions. They were fighting for survival.

At first I was surprised that my more experienced coworkers told me to drive the garbage truck. Then I realized that they were expert garbage pickers who often found things that they could use or sell along the route. There was also the fact that during the holidays, many of our customers left "tips" in the form of cash in envelopes or cans of beer. The driver of the garbage truck didn't get to share in that loot.

I didn't mind. Working on the garbage truck and doing hard manual labor educated me about the realities of the workplace. I saw how Mr. Conger, a successful entrepreneur with a college education, lived, and although he too worked long hours, there was just no comparing the quality of his life to that of the guys on the garbage truck.

When I was 16, Mr. Conger helped me start my first business, Shallenberger Maintenance Company. He invited me to his house one day to discuss the start-up. I drove to his beautiful, huge house, and as I went up his driveway, I saw two matching Cadillacs with personalized plates that said, "Conger 1" and "Conger 2." I had never seen anything so luxurious. I thought: *I like this. I think I can do this.*

That was an "aha" moment for me. I realized that Mr. Conger had been able to create a wonderful life beyond anything that I could have imagined because he had prepared himself for opportunities by getting an education and applying his knowledge in the real world of business.

My attitude toward school and education was transformed that year. Before that, I'd been a poor student, mostly because I lacked motivation. Now I had it. My upbringing in humble circumstances and my experiences with the garbage guys and other blue-collar workers left me with a great respect and empathy for them. They were good people who were working hard to make ends meet. However, my work with Mr. Conger opened my eyes to what greater opportunities there were for people who were willing to obtain knowledge and put it to work in their lives.

Are you satisfied with your progress in your career? Are your relationships as fulfilling as you'd like them to be? Do you feel that there is something greater you could be doing with your life if you just had the necessary information and the ability to apply it?

This guiding constant can be one of the greatest game changers in your life or in the lives of your employees. The tools I'll discuss in this chapter can help you answer all these questions. They can open a pathway to becoming your best in each area of your life.

Lead with the Power of Knowledge

A number of years ago, two of our sons were cadets at the U.S. Air Force Academy. During the parents' weekend, we were provided with a tour of the beautiful campus, nestled in the foothills of the Rocky Mountains. On the main quad, I stood in front of a large statue depicting a falcon and her chick; the inscription at the base of the statue reads, "Man's flight through life is sustained by the power of his knowledge." The inscription uses words like *flight*, *sustained*, and *power* in relation to *knowledge*. Indeed, one can be lifted and flight can be sustained by the power of knowledge.

The wings of knowledge and enlightenment can help you soar to great heights in your personal life, in your relationships, and at work. The lack of knowledge leaves you on the ground and at times renders you defenseless against the forces of the external environment.

The fact is that your actions and your behavior follow your thoughts. If you thoughtfully engineer *what* goes into your mind and your heart, these factors of change will have an enormous impact on your ability to achieve your dreams and realize the best you can be.

> "As a single footstep will not make a path on the earth, so a single thought will not make a pathway in the mind. To make a deep physical path, we walk again and again. To make a deep mental path, we must think over and over the kind of thoughts we wish to dominate our lives."
>
> —Henry David Thoreau

As you travel this journey toward your best, be a positive catalyst in that journey. Share the excitement of learning with those who are interested. Those who associate with you will feel the power of growth; even if you don't say anything, the impact of your journey will radiate from within you.

Think of your arm. As you curl it and flex your muscle, what happens to your biceps? When you work out and really make an effort to develop your muscles, they get stronger and grow. Your mind is like a muscle. If you don't stretch or stimulate it, it can atrophy and become weak.

With knowledge and experience comes wisdom. Wisdom allows us to make better use of our knowledge. This process of gaining knowledge allows one to see things more clearly and with a better understanding.

I was teaching a group of executives, and I asked them what the qualities are of a great learner. They came up with a few answers, including *hungry to learn, desirous of knowledge, attentive, prepared*, and *humble*.

These are all important qualities of an effective learner. It's interesting that these attributes are also some of the most important qualities for leaders. Among the qualities expressed, perhaps humility is the most important. Humility allows each one of us to be open to new thoughts and ideas, without letting prejudiced or preconceived ideas get in the way of our learning.

If we really want to learn to apply the power of knowledge, it's important that we approach learning with those characteristics: a hunger to learn, humility, and a willingness to try new things.

> "Take the attitude of a student, never
> be too big to ask questions, never know
> too much to learn something new."
>
> —Og Mandino

In the spirit of learning together, let's look at three dynamic ways in which we can continuously grow through knowledge:

1. Stimulate and exercise the mind.

2. Regularly assess the external environment.

3. Invite and get feedback.

Stimulate and Exercise the Mind

About 35 years ago, my friend Charlie Jones shared a quote with me that rocked my world.

> "You will be the same person in five years
> as you are today, except for two things: the
> people you meet and the books you read."
>
> —Charlie "Tremendous" Jones

The message of this quote is powerfully accurate because the quality of your life is directly affected by the choices you make. Even when a setback or tragedy strikes, the knowledge you have acquired from the people you have met and the books you have read can help you overcome it and move forward to be your best. In order to apply knowledge, though, you must first acquire it.

Take a moment to ponder this question: What do you or your organization want to be like in five years? Once you have that vision formed in your mind, what can you do to get to that point? What principles and thoughts should you cultivate?

As you build upon what you have already accomplished and cultivate your unique qualities, seek to associate with people and read books that will move you closer to your best. It's also essential that you avoid negative conversations and books that could keep you from your goals—and that could possibly destroy your dreams.

If you are on top of your game today, what will represent your better or best in the next five years? If you are broke, sick, or stuck, or if you feel like a failure, you can still begin right now to get on track; it's never too late. You can make the decision and take the actions that will put you in a better place one day, one week, one month, and five years from now. So determine now that you will surround yourself with people who can help you get to a better place and that you will acquire the knowledge you need if you are to become the best you can be.

After reading Charlie's quote for the first time, I found myself thinking about the things that I hoped to accomplish in the next five years. After I had a vision of where I wanted to be, I thought about the books that could provide the information necessary to achieve my goals. I also considered the people who would make a difference and increase my knowledge. This simple formula transformed my life.

Where would *you* like to be in five years?

Remember, Charlie started by saying that we'll be the same in five years except for the people we meet and the books we read. Let's look at Charlie's quote a little more closely. I have several game-changing invitations that could have a dramatic impact on your personal and professional life:

- Develop the habit of reading at least one book a month.

- Invest 3 percent of your income in acquiring more knowledge through seminars, training, books, and personal development courses.

- Surround yourself with people who inspire and lift you.

The goal is to become the best you can be, to reach the highest income level you want to attain, and to create the most fulfilling life you can imagine. So, the books you read should be those that teach you new skills, increase your knowledge, and help you grow in your professional and relationship skills. It might be helpful to keep a journal of reflections on what you've read, as this will help you to retain knowledge and information. Ask yourself, how can the key points in the book be applied to my life? After all, what you know isn't of value until you apply it.

Many authors pour their life experiences into their books so that others can benefit from them. Reading, then, is a way to hyperaccelerate your development by learning from the successes and failures—and the research—of accomplished men and women. I've found that highly successful leaders almost always read voraciously.

I once attended a sales seminar in which the speaker invited his audience to read at least a book a month. In this case, the invitation was to read a book on the subject of increasing sales production. He insisted that reading such a book each month could help sales professionals double their sales in a year.

One participant took him up on this challenge, and did in fact double his sales year after year for three years. As he moved into the fourth year, however, his sales started to decline, and he couldn't figure out why. Then he realized that he had stopped reading a book a month about halfway through his third year. It was an "aha" moment for him. He immediately resumed reading a book a month, and once he did that, his sales and his income rose again.

I don't believe that's just a coincidence. I've witnessed this type of example over and over again with people who read about how to become their best in whatever field they're in.

Read Books and Reap the Rewards

When you read at least one book a month, you reap many benefits. You stimulate your mind. You acquire more knowledge and enhance your skill sets. The brain is like a computer. When you try to access a file that's not in the computer, you get an error message that says, "File not found." When you read and learn from others, you're loading the files into your mind so that you can access them when you need them.

I began reading at least one book a month a few years ago, and it changed my life. Since then, I've informally polled many of the most successful people I've known, and the majority of them said that they try to follow the same routine to keep their minds sharp. Reading a book a month takes effort and discipline, which are traits that are found in successful men and women.

What is an area of your life that you would like to improve? Are you interested in improving the quality of your relationships or becoming a better parent, a better salesperson, a better customer service rep, or a better CEO? Now, make a list of books you can read that would help achieve your goals in whatever area you chose.

Invest 3 Percent of Your Income in Yourself

Now for the second part of the equation to stimulate and exercise your mind: invest 3 percent of your income in yourself.

While at dinner recently, I shared this advice, and a lady asked with a big smile, "Does that mean a pedicure?" I laughed and realized that I should clarify what I mean when I suggest that you invest 3 percent of your income in yourself. And no, gentlemen, it also does not mean that you should buy yourself a new car.

This is money that you put into expanding your mind and your knowledge.

One person I know followed this plan while starting his career. The first year, he could put in only about $500, which was 3 percent of his income. After almost five years, he had increased his income so rapidly that when he calculated what 3 percent of his income would be, he was amazed. His income had risen by several hundred percent in just a few years.

He has stayed with the 3 percent plan and has experienced great success and increased his income each year. Imagine what this type of increase would do for you and your organization. Imagine what it would be like if your income or your sales figures doubled each year. Every person I know who has followed this plan has experienced substantial success. If you do this, you'll probably see a dramatic improvement in many different areas of your life. I've personally followed this principle for years, and it never ceases to amaze me that so many powerful and impactful ideas are generated, both personally and professionally.

> "The more things you try, the more likely one of them will work. The more books you read, the more likely one of them will have an answer to a question that could solve the major problems of your life."
>
> —Jack Canfield

What would 3 percent of your income amount to? Think about ways you could invest that in being a better leader or sales manager, becoming more physically fit, developing stronger relationships, or learning skills that make you more valuable in your career. Are there some courses you could take that might help in a particular area, such as motivation, sales training, personal growth, emotional intelligence, leadership skills, or relationships?

Invest in Success

This doesn't just apply to individuals; it applies to businesses as well. There are numerous studies that show a direct correlation between organizations that invest in their employees and the company's bottom line. The challenge for an executive is to view this as an investment, rather than an expense. Typically a person will cut expenses, but not investments. I've met and associated with many business leaders who wholeheartedly believe in investing in their most important resource: their employees. Research shows that those executives who invest in their people will reap the rewards of their investment to include more loyal employees, increased profitability, lower turnover, increased customer satisfaction, better leaders, and a stronger organization. I've met many business leaders who told me they wished that they would have made time and started investing in their employees sooner because of the enormous positive impact that training had within their organization.

Surround Yourself with People Who Inspire You

In addition to reading at least a book a month and investing 3 percent of your income in yourself, another way to stimulate and exercise the mind is to create or join a mastermind group. Throughout my life, I've benefited from having amazing individuals serve on the advisory boards of companies that I owned or led. This has been an extraordinary experience for me as well as for the other associates of our companies.

I have been involved with many forums and mastermind groups over the years. For the past 30 years, I've participated in a monthly forum with a dozen CEOs. These associations have allowed me to run many of my ideas by these people to get fresh perspectives, gain from their collective experiences and wisdom, and—sometimes—get shot down in private, which is better than making a costly mistake in the real world.

When looking for wise minds to consult, you should find a group of people who inspire and motivate you. Finding others who want you to succeed isn't easy, but the benefits are worth the hunt. I suggest that you look around in your local area and find a way to join or form such an advisory group. The idea is to surround yourself with people who can help you be your best.

Maybe you could also consider investing in a coach who can help you review your vision and your goals, then chart a course to get there. If you take this route, make sure that the coach has strong credentials and references. A great coach can be a valuable asset and guide you to higher achievements and greater fulfillment, but some coaches are more qualified than others. You don't want to waste your time or your money. If you invest in a coach, do what my friend, the entrepreneur and motivational speaker James Malinchak, suggested, "Find someone who's been there and done that and is still doing it successfully!"

We recently witnessed the power of coaching and investing in yourself when one of my sons attended a training and speaking conference. He called from the event and said that he'd learned about a well-regarded coaching program and wanted some of our team members to enroll. The price was not inexpensive—$15,000 a year, with a 10 percent discount for investing the entire amount up front.

Fortunately, we made the investment, and it has paid off in several ways. As part of the program, we've joined several mastermind groups and met other amazing people who have proved to be great resources. This investment will have a positive ripple effect for many years. The good news is that creating a mastermind group doesn't have to cost a penny. It can be as simple as asking someone you admire to act as an informal advisor to help you define and achieve your goals. Offer to send this person a written report at the end of the year, showing your progress.

You might want to take the members of your mastermind group to lunch or dinner now and then. Make sure you are careful about the people you recruit because you don't want to be confiding in someone whom you can't trust. Who can you think of that fits the profile? You need someone who is wise and inspiring—a good listener with an abundance mentality who will want you to succeed. Make a list of potential mastermind advisors and then offer to take them to lunch one at a time so that you can present your idea to them.

It's all about stimulating your mind to reach great heights. It's about reading books and building relationships with people who can help you pursue your dreams and become your best.

Of all the things we teach, this particular bit of advice has been one of the most fruitful and one of the greatest game changers in my life. To summarize, you can grow and stimulate your mind by reading a book a month, investing 3 percent of your income in your own development each year, and joining or creating an inspiring group. These are proven methods for acquiring the necessary knowledge to soar to amazing new heights in many different areas of your life.

Here is the second part of this principle.

Regularly Assess the External Environment

One thing that is certain is this: change is constant. The things that worked yesterday may not work tomorrow. Forces and events are constantly changing. The forces of change are so dynamic in our lives that if we aren't continuously thinking about them, it could put us, and our organizations, at great risk.

I call these forces of change the external environment. When I say "external environment," I am usually referring to things that are outside of your control (see Figure 10.1). They include natural disasters, disease, the death of a loved one, an accident, the economy, government regulations, your spouse or partner, children,

FIGURE 10.1 The External Environment

people you work with, setbacks with your company, competition, changing markets, and bad weather. If you're standing on the tracks, you need to know if there's a train coming!

I recommend that you make an assessment of your external environment regularly. I do this at least once a quarter. It is as simple as getting out a clean sheet of paper and drawing a large circle as illustrated. You are on the inside, and the external environment is on the outside.

Now, write down all of the external forces on the outside that could possibly have an impact on your life. Many of the forces that we have already discussed may be on that list.

Take a second and think about all the forces that exist in your external environment. Has there been anything in your genes that might give you a propensity toward a certain health problem, such as cancer, eye problems, or heart disease? Do you have multiple suppliers, or do you rely on one supplier? If you have only one supplier, what would happen if a natural disaster disrupted that supplier's operations? These are just a couple of questions that might help to get you started.

If you are concerned about a specific health issue, then you can identify something you can do about it to avoid a serious health problem. We've used this technique many times in our organization, and it has saved us from some big losses.

Once you finish thinking about the various factors, circle or highlight the two or three threats or opportunities that can have the biggest impact on your life. Then develop an action plan for taking advantage of opportunities or avoiding the threats to you and your organization.

This exercise can contribute to personal success, relationship success, or the success of an organization, and it can save a lot of heartache. It can help you identify potential opportunities by observing trends. It helps you think ahead—3 months, 12 months, 5 years, and 10 years down the road. It is a great "what-if" exercise. This is key to your success. You need to be constantly aware of the threats and opportunities that are coming at you.

This is a powerful way to gain knowledge, which then allows you to effectively apply it.

Now we'll discuss the third key to applying the power of knowledge.

Invite and Get Feedback

A wealth of knowledge is available to you. If you are willing to receive feedback and use it as an improvement tool, it can open your eyes to specific things you can do that will make you more effective. Feedback is all around you; all you have to do is ask for it. This is free consulting! Sometimes it's just about getting your ego out of the way.

Wheaties called its cereal the "Breakfast of Champions." It's also safe to say, "*Feedback* is the Breakfast of Champions."

Having the ability to accept feedback and to correct your direction or decisions is a key element of becoming a champion in any area of your life. Champions know that success is inevitable, and that failure is best accepted as feedback leading to further improvement. There are a couple of effective keys to gaining knowledge through feedback. The first is to assemble a network of people who will provide honest, insightful opinions about what you are doing. The second is to know how to solicit and accept feedback through questions. You might ask, "Honey, does this tie work with this jacket?" or, "The focus group data says that this product will be a winner. What are we missing that could trip us up? What's out there that we don't see that could derail us and wipe out the success we are anticipating?"

Your feedback network should be made up of people you respect. It should include people who have experience and can be trusted to be honest about your performance, your relationship with your children, and the company's strategy or the product's potential. Treat them well, because they are worth their weight in gold. You can use your mastermind group for this purpose, too.

You can also do an exercise that doesn't require others to be present. It's a virtual feedback network. This is about tapping into your own conscious and subconscious mind. In your mind's eye, imagine that you are seated at a round boardroom table with a number of great minds. Shut your eyes and ask your imaginary advisors, "What would you recommend?" "What would you do, Mr. Gandhi, Ms. Keller, Mr. Edison, Mr. Lincoln, Mr. Churchill, Ms. Winfrey or whoever is in your meeting?" Listen carefully to the responses from your subconscious mind.

Take just a minute and ask yourself, who are some of the most influential people in history who could sit in your boardroom and give you feedback? The next time you have a challenging question, I invite you to close your eyes and envision each of these people providing you with feedback concerning your challenge or plan.

Be prepared to accept feedback. Shut off your tendency to be offended or hurt when someone criticizes or fails to lavish praise on your latest idea. Be quick to listen, humble, open, and willing to learn from others. Refuse to deal out blame. Highly successful leaders are humble enough to solicit and receive feedback.

Whether you're getting feedback in a real group setting or using feedback from your virtual network, carefully consider the counsel you receive. That's what wise people do. I've seen one of them in action.

While I was serving on the board of directors of Covey Leadership Center, some very hot issues would sometimes surface. My friend, the late Stephen R. Covey, was chairman of the board. Even when he was opposed to some of the ideas that came up, he always amazed me by sitting up in his chair with genuine interest and saying, "I would love to know more about why you feel the way you do. Would you mind sharing with me your thoughts on this?" He would then carefully weigh what he had heard.

Feedback is a powerful way to get valuable information. Whether you're in a family or an organization, you should create a culture of feedback and open communication. Foster feedback by complimenting those who give it and taking it into account in visible ways. You can make it okay to provide feedback by giving positive responses.

Another simple, yet extremely powerful way to give and receive feedback is the Continue–Start–Stop tool. This is the same tool I discussed in Chapter 7. It's such a valuable tool, I'm going to briefly review it again here. The Continue–Start–Stop is a single sheet of paper with three questions on it.

1. Continue: "What should I (or the company) continue doing?"

2. Start: "What should I (or the company) start doing?"

3. Stop: "What should I (or the company) stop doing?"

You can use this tool with coworkers, customers, your spouse, or even a child. We suggest using it with all your employees or the members of your team. One of the keys to using Continue–Start–Stop is asking participants to be specific. If someone suggests that people be more kind, that's not something you can easily act on as a leader of an organization. However, if someone suggests taking

15 minutes a week to recognize the lessons learned and take steps to incorporate them, that's actionable and specific. Invite people to be specific when doing this exercise.

We periodically pass out Continue–Start–Stop sheets to all our employees. I just love the anonymous feedback. It is so healthy and so necessary. When we did this recently, I noticed that there was a need for better communication between certain departments. The managers of those departments immediately got together and came up with some great strategies and a plan of action for improving communication. The Continue–Start–Stop is a powerful, yet simple tool that anyone can use to give and receive feedback.

Formal and Informal Feedback

Asking for suggestions and advice sometimes can be best done in informal settings. You can ask questions while driving to a meeting, while flying to a conference, or over lunch.

"How can we improve our associates' training?"

"What does *the best* look like for the company? For the group?"

Informal feedback is useful for collecting information on processes, product development, strategy development, and even the skills needed by new hires. Opinions of all kinds inform our thinking and provide reality checks for the direction in which various activities are going.

Feedback from your family or your coworkers is not necessarily collected through a survey. That is why "management by walking around" can be so valuable. On the other hand, simple surveys such as Continue–Start–Stop can be also very useful.

Remember, the only surefire way to gain knowledge is to seek it. People who seek knowledge through feedback and are willing to accept it will benefit greatly. This is a very powerful tool that we all have access to.

Ways to Apply the Power of Knowledge

We've looked at several ways of building and applying knowledge:

1. Read a book a month and keep a journal of the key points.

2. Invest 3 percent of your income in yourself.

3. Start or join a mastermind group.

4. Regularly assess the external environment.

5. Search for feedback and willingly accept it.

Leadership Lessons of Socrates

When you think of this guiding concept, keep this story in mind. A young man approached Socrates as he sat by a lake. The young man told Socrates that he would do anything to gain the wisdom Socrates possessed.

After a moment, Socrates stood up and motioned for the young man to follow him. He walked into the lake until he was waist deep in the water. Then Socrates asked the young man what he really wanted. When the young man insisted that he wanted wisdom, Socrates pushed the young man's head under the water.

The man struggled and finally surfaced, wondering what the philosopher was up to. Again, Socrates asked him what he wanted. The man responded, "Wisdom." Again Socrates shoved his head under water. The man struggled longer before finally coming up for air.

For the third time, Socrates asked the man what he really wanted. When he pushed his head under water this time, Socrates held it there for almost a minute. The man finally fought his way up, gasping for air.

At that moment, Socrates asked him, "What is it you want?" This time the man was honest. He said, "I want air!" Socrates smiled and responded, "When you want wisdom as much as you wanted that breath of air, you won't need me, and you shall get it."

So it is with knowledge. When you hunger and thirst for knowledge as much as you want air, you will get it.

"We have a hunger of the mind which asks
for knowledge of all around us, and the more
we gain, the more is our desire; the more we
see, the more we are capable of seeing."
—Maria Mitchell

I promise that when you are armed with knowledge and apply it with all the energy and enthusiasm you have, it changes the game. It helps you to develop creative new ideas and solutions, to scale new heights, and to see new vistas. Knowledge will provide you with an enormous competitive edge that makes a decisive difference in a rapidly changing world.

Leadership Action Steps

1. Hunger and thirst for knowledge. Read, meet, associate, and observe. Remember that in five years, you will be the same as you are today except for the people you meet and the books you read.

2. Examine the external environment regularly. Change—the external environment—can provide you with valuable opportunities or drown you in its wake. Use the external environment analysis tool to your advantage.

3. Look at what's going on in innovation and research. What's out there now? What does the best look like? Who has succeeded? Who has failed? Who has used search tools? What is the baseline or benchmark?

4. Read at least one book a month that teaches you how to improve in some way. Remember, leaders are readers.

5. Invest 3 percent of your income in developing your mind, talents, and skills.

6. Form a mastermind group or forum: a group of people whom you trust and respect.

7. Ask for and be open to feedback. Feedback is the breakfast of champions.

8. Use the Continue–Start–Stop tool to obtain feedback.

9. Work hard to think clearly and understand the real causes and effects of events and situations. Don't jump to conclusions.

10. Get the facts or leave it alone or the conclusions you come to may be your own.

CHAPTER 11

Live in Peace and Balance

Radiate a peaceful, strong, and positive light from within.

There was once a king who offered a prize to the artist who could paint the best picture of peace. Many artists tried, and the king looked at all the pictures. After deliberating for several days, he had narrowed down his choices to two. He had to choose between them.

One picture was of a calm lake. The lake was a perfect mirror for the peaceful mountains that towered around it. Overhead, fluffy white clouds floated in a blue sky. Everyone who saw this picture said that it was the perfect picture of peace.

The second picture had mountains as well. However, these mountains were rugged and bare. Above them was an angry gray sky from which rain was falling. Lightning flashed. A foaming waterfall tumbled down the side of the mountain. This certainly didn't appear to be a peaceful place.

But when the king looked at the picture more closely, he saw that behind the waterfall, a tiny bush was growing in the rock. Inside the bush, a mother bird had built her nest.

There, in the midst of the rush of angry water, sat the mother bird on her nest. She was the perfect picture of peace.

The king chose the second picture.

"Because," he explained, "peace is not only in a place where there is no noise, trouble, or hard work. Peace is in the midst of things as they are, when there is calm in your heart. That is the real meaning of peace."

Not many people can claim to be free of worry and stress, but there are ways to find peace and balance in the midst of chaos and the daily rush of life. You can find peace and balance each and every day. You don't have to wait until all your challenges and stresses have passed. Peace is always yours to claim.

In our research, we found that 30 percent of employees feel that they are completely burned out or stressed by their jobs, and nearly 40 percent feel that they've used up all their energy at the end of each workday. Certainly this will vary by industry, but think about the effect of these feelings on production and employee turnover! What if you could lower those effects and reduce turnover?

> "The only way to bring peace to the earth is
> to learn to make our own life peaceful."
> —The Buddha

Business leaders are more successful when they help their employees learn how to manage stress and increase their balance. If leaders can do that, they're likely to reduce employee turnover and increase productivity. It is also helpful for you and your team members to have a positive environment and culture in which they can thrive and feel fulfilled so that everyone looks forward to coming to work each day. Fortunately, there are some things that highly successful leaders can do to find greater peace and balance in their work and personal lives.

Four Steps to Finding Peace amid Turmoil

These four harmonizing principles of peace and balance can help you clear your mind during even the most chaotic times at work or at home. They can be especially helpful to leaders who are striving for the highest levels of success.

1. Increase balance in your life.

2. Increase your peace through meditation.

3. Laugh often.

4. See yourself in a positive light through self-affirmation and positive self-talk.

Let's look at each of these harmonizing principles in depth.

Increase Balance in Your Life

The first step in finding peace is to increase balance in our personal lives. This may sound easy, but achieving it takes effort and discipline. *Forbes* magazine wrote about a survey of 3,500 managers around the world conducted by the global management-consulting firm Booz & Company. The survey showed that a striking majority of corporate leaders have difficulty keeping their priorities straight and their lives in balance. Of those surveyed, nearly 64 percent said that their biggest frustration was dealing with conflicting priorities.

Balance is important for everyone, from top executives to line employees and those working in the home. The late motivational speaker Zig Ziglar said, "Being successful means having a balance of success stories across the many areas of your life. You can't truly be considered successful in your business life if your home life is in shambles."

Sometimes we get so caught up in our work that our personal lives suffer, and sometimes personal problems can overwhelm us to such an extent that we are no longer effective in our work. We may not be aware that our lives are out of balance until a great deal of damage has been done or things have skidded out of control.

It's like driving a car with a bad tire. You may not notice it at first, but then the steering wheel pulls one way or another, or the car rattles and shimmies until you have difficulty staying on the road. A few years ago, I was driving to a ski resort with my family when the car ran over a large rock that seemed to have come out of nowhere. It was a bumpy ride after that.

Every crack or dip in the road caused the drinks in our cup holders to slosh. The car rumbled and bounced. Clearly, there was something seriously wrong with the tire that had hit the rock. I had to get it repaired and have the tires rebalanced to prevent a blowout.

A tire on a car can run for many miles with the wheel out of balance, but sooner or later, it will fail. Similarly, you may be able to focus on one area of your life at the expense of another for some time, but if your life is out of balance, you run the risk of a blowout sooner or later.

When our car's wheels and tires are in proper working condition, they can last a long time and run for thousands of miles. When our lives are in balance, we feel fulfilled and at peace, and we're likely to live longer and be happier.

Finding peace and balance requires inner strength. The more self-reliant and balanced you are in the different areas of your life, the greater your capacity to work effectively while making a difference.

The Circle of Peace and Balance

Let's try a simple assessment called the *Circle of Peace and Balance*, shown in Figure 11.1. The Circle of Peace and Balance divides our lives into six areas that need our attention and consistent care. When each of these six areas is properly cared for, it's like balancing the wheels on your car to keep it running smoothly.

I invite you to rate yourself in each area on a scale of 1 to 10. A rating of 1 means that you haven't given that area any attention or you feel that it's been neglected. A 10 rating means that things couldn't be better in that area of your life.

The first area in the Circle of Peace and Balance deals with your physical and emotional health. This area might include the amount of exercise you get, your overall sense of well-being, your

FIGURE 11.1 The Circle of Peace and Balance

stress levels, the quality of your sleep, and whether you have a healthy diet.

The second area focuses on your mental health and your intellect. Are you working to develop and cultivate your mind? Are you constantly building your knowledge and staying mentally sharp? This includes exercising your brain and maintaining a positive attitude.

The third area deals with the financial aspects of your life. Most people who are financially sound follow wise practices in handling their money. They maintain a balance between what they earn and what they spend. They have savings plans. They also avoid debt, invest wisely, maintain emergency reserves, and provide for their retirement years.

Security and safety are covered in the fourth area. When you focus on living a secure and safe life, you don't take unnecessary risks. You prepare for the future, ensuring that those you love will be protected if anything should happen to you.

Social life and relationships are the focus of the fifth area. Here, you review the quality of your relationships with your family, friends, and coworkers and with those in your community.

The last area of the circle involves your spiritual life. When you cultivate a tenderness and sensitivity toward others, you feed your spirit. The same is true when you help those in need, treat others as you would like to be treated, and generally try to make the world a better place.

With all these elements in place, the Circle of Peace and Balance resembles a wheel with six spokes. Each spoke of the wheel represents one of the six areas that are critical to maintaining balance in your life. To determine whether you are doing that, rate yourself on a scale of 1 to 10 in each of the six areas and circle that number.

After you've rated yourself, connect the dots (the numbers that you circled). If you have a nice balanced circle, congratulations! However, most people rate themselves high in some areas and not so high in other areas. When they've connected the dots,

FIGURE 11.2 **An Unbalanced Circle**

the circle is not perfectly round; it is slightly out of alignment. Figure 11.2 gives a simple example of what such a circle might look like.

Apply the Circle of Peace and Balance

Remember the tire analogy: if your life is not in balance, you may cruise along for a while, but eventually problems will occur, and a breakdown may be inevitable. Think about these areas in your own life: mental, financial, security and safety, relationships, spiritual, and your physical and emotional health. After doing this exercise and rating yourself, consider whether there are any areas in your life that could use more time and attention. Ask yourself what you can do each day to give those areas more attention.

Recently, a woman in one of our seminars realized that she wasn't devoting enough time to her physical health. Inspired by the Circle of Peace and Balance, she set a goal of living a properly balanced, healthier life. With her new priorities established, she came up with a workout and eating plan.

After just four months, she had lost 40 pounds! In addition, her job performance had significantly improved. Before doing this simple exercise, she was just an average employee, but after making these adjustments, she became a highly successful leader in her company. According to her, she had more energy, and she found a renewed enthusiasm for her work and her life. This one simple exercise opened up a world of possibilities for her. Because of her transformation, she also served as an inspiration for her supervisors and peers at work.

In another case I witnessed, a CEO who was also a physician completed the Circle of Peace and Balance exercise during one of our seminars. After doing so, he realized that his health had seriously deteriorated in the previous year because he had devoted so much time and energy to his business. He often felt sick and stressed. He told me that as a result of our seminar, he had made some serious adjustments in his life and his priorities.

"Not until I did this exercise did I realize how out of balance my life had become," he said. "For the first time, I realized that if I continued at the pace I was going at, I might die 10 to 20 years prematurely. I was focusing so much on my work that it was costing me my health and my family!"

The Circle of Peace and Balance is a simple way to assess whether your life is in balance, but make no mistake, it can be a lifesaver if you use it to identify areas that may need additional attention. Once you identify those areas, you can go to work and make the necessary adjustments.

The second way of putting your life in harmony through peace and balance that we recommend is meditation, which has become increasingly accepted in both the workplace and the home. It has been around for centuries, of course. In the past, it has been much more prevalent in Asian countries, but today you can find meditation being practiced in corporations and at local YMCAs. Let's take a look.

Increase Your Peace Through Meditation

Research has shown that taking a few moments during the day to relax or meditate can return significant dividends in your performance and effectiveness.

What do you envision when you think of meditation? Before I learned more about this valuable tool, I imagined that meditation was something done by monks on mountaintops, sitting cross-legged and rising magically off their mats.

I've since learned that meditation is much more down-to-earth and a wonderful stress reduction tool. Sometimes it can be as simple as pushing back from your desk in the middle of the day, taking a couple of minutes to visualize a relaxing image, breathe deeply, and open your mind to reflect on positive thoughts.

Meditation can be a powerful tool to use anywhere, but it can be especially effective in the workplace. You can do it in a couple of minutes or you can take longer, depending on your preferences and your timetable. I've benefited from meditation even when it just meant taking a brief pause at work to refocus and reenergize.

Even the U.S. Marines are studying meditation techniques as a way to focus and energize their men and women in the field. As I've mentioned previously, two of my sons are fighter pilots, and they use meditation to calm their minds in preparation for their intense and demanding missions. In fact, they are trained to recognize when they are in danger of becoming overstressed so that they can take steps to calm themselves and clear their minds.

Task Saturation Signals a Need for Meditation

It's a little ironic that meditation is most useful at those times when you are stressed out and under the gun—those times when you feel that you have no time to spare. How do you recognize when it's time to step back for a few minutes? Who better to ask than a couple of guys who have what is arguably among the most intense and nerve-wracking job on the planet?

Part of the training my sons received as fighter pilots was to recognize when they have reached the point of "task saturation." These are moments when you have way too much to do, and you don't have the time, tools, or resources to get it all done—the point at which you feel that you're on the edge of cracking up or shutting down.

Task saturation comes fast and furiously when you are hurtling through the skies at 600 miles per hour with hundreds of instruments to monitor, listening to radio calls, keeping wingmen in formation, and dealing with weather, terrain, weaponry, and, of course, enemy aircraft. These intense situations require unbelievable self-control because if just one of the high-priority tasks falls through the cracks, the results can be deadly. As task saturation increases, performance decreases and errors in execution increase—not a good formula.

While most jobs are not as intense as flying jet fighters, you should be able to recognize when you're starting to get task saturated in your own job, so that you can make adjustments to calm yourself, clear your mind, and prioritize. You probably know the feeling—for example, when e-mails start piling up, the deadline for an important project is approaching, and your spouse calls to ask if you can pick something up on the way home. It's that feeling of being overwhelmed.

Fighter pilots are carefully trained to prevent disasters in the air by recognizing the warning signs of task saturation and refocusing their minds on their top priorities in each situation. When pilots feel that they are beginning to get task saturated, they are trained to mentally step back and focus on the most important priorities. They shed the tasks that aren't as important and focus on the top priorities. Then, as they come back into balance and the stress is reduced, they can add additional tasks.

How to Combat Task Saturation in Your World

As I mentioned earlier, Air Force pilots aren't the only ones who experience task saturation. You might have five customers in line, two phones on hold, your kid's teacher calling to say that she's sick, and your manager waiting for a report that's an hour late. Whether you are a CEO, a midlevel manager with many responsibilities, or a parent who is scrambling to keep your family afloat, you can find yourself stressed out when there is too much going on and too little time to deal with it.

You can apply the same methods that fighter pilots use to your own task saturation moments. When you feel overwhelmed by a myriad of responsibilities that require immediate attention, follow the procedures that work for these pilots. Physically or mentally step back, close your eyes, control your breathing, and establish your priorities as your mind clears.

Once you've been able to calm your mind and determine what's most important, then you can reengage with your activities without the stress and panicked feelings that come with task saturation. Once the most important things are under control, you can add responsibilities one at a time until you are comfortably doing everything that you need to do.

Think about your own experience. When have you felt overwhelmed to the point of task saturation? Wouldn't stepping back for just a few minutes, controlling your breathing, and clearing your mind have helped you be more effective? The goal of these relaxation methods is to improve your performance. You can't become your best when you feel that you are under siege, and, unlike fighter pilots, you can't pull the ejection handle and bail out when things get completely out of control.

There are several different ways to meditate to counter task saturation and the stress that comes with it. Let's look at some techniques that can be very effective, both at home and in the workplace.

A Becoming Your Best Exercise: The Five Basic Steps of Meditation

I invite you to try this basic meditation exercise. After you have done so, you can create your own style of meditation based on your circumstances. The first step is to close your eyes, so please make sure that you are in a safe and secure environment.

1. Close your eyes and relax.

2. Take several deep breaths. Fill your lungs completely and exhale fully. Feel the heaviness of your hands, arms, and legs lighten as you let them totally relax.

3. Imagine a serene, safe, and peaceful location. Use your mind's eye to find a place that is inviting, warm, and comfortable.

4. When you arrive at this place, focus or reflect on any of the areas of the Circle of Peace and Balance to find answers to your questions or concerns.

    You may choose to simply focus on an issue that concerns you. If it is health-related, your body frequently has the answers. Your body can teach you a great deal—you need only ask it. Occasionally you may fall asleep, which means that you need rest. Avoid mental multitasking by focusing on only one area during each "visit" to your inner counselor.

5. You can take as much time as you need, or you can do this in as little as three or four minutes. If you're able to, pause and take a few minutes to give this a try and see how it feels. After reflection and meditation, you will find that you typically feel more at peace. You may find that your body is more relaxed, your mind is more focused, and your soul is more energized.

What are some ways that you can do this type of exercise throughout the day, even if it's only for a couple of minutes? You don't want meditation time to cut into your work time; rather, it should increase your effectiveness at work. You can meditate several times a day if you like. I encourage you to find at least one time outside of work each week when you can get a full 10 to 20 minutes of uninterrupted meditation. Use that time to relax and free up your mind.

In our fast-paced culture, finding the time for these moments of meditation and reflection is difficult, yet doing so is vital if you really want to find peace. This becomes especially useful in moments when you are task saturated. It can help you refocus on the highest-priority items and then go to work without the bombarding stress that can overwhelm you.

A Becoming Your Best Exercise: Chair Flying— Another Form of Meditation

Before a flight, the most successful fighter pilots take between 10 and 15 minutes to go over the most important details of the mission in their mind's eye. They create the exact situation, the sights and sounds, to make it as real as possible. They mentally go through the motions of moving the throttle to the required position, identify the target location and note what it would look like from the air, establish where the wingman will be, and walk through the countdown to weapons release and the preweapons checks.

Visualizing and mentally going through a flight is called *chair flying*. It's a powerful form of meditation, and anybody can do it. Imagine taking a few minutes before a sales call, an important meeting with a key client, or a presentation to your team to briefly chair fly what you will be doing before you do the real thing.

These meditation techniques are simple and practical for everyday use, yet they can make a big difference in your effectiveness in the workplace and at home. We tend to be far more successful leaders when our minds are clear and focused. Meditation and visualization are accepted and proven methods that can help you find peace, reduce stress, regain your energy and excitement, and take control of your life. And unlike my sons, you won't need a parachute for backup!

Laugh Often

The third aspect to live in peace and balance throughout your life is to laugh often. Laughter and a sense of humor are infectious. The sound of laughter is far more contagious than a flu bug and, unlike the flu, when laughter is shared, it bonds people and tends to increase their happiness.

Laughter triggers healthy physical responses in your body. It strengthens your immune system, increases your energy, reduces your pain, and relieves stress. Humor can lighten your burdens, brighten your spirits, inspire hope, connect you to others, and help you stay focused. Well-placed and tasteful humor helps create a constructive environment.

If they are applied at the right time, laughter and a good sense of humor can change a tense situation to one that is more inviting and relaxed. Humor can completely change the tone of a meeting so that the participants can put things into perspective more easily and move on to a positive solution.

I've seen this many times thanks to my friend Gardner, a successful businessman who has developed a rare gift for creating laughter in the middle of tense situations. During meetings I have attended, Gardner often found the perfect time to unleash humorous stories. For example, during a meeting in which many people were trying to assert themselves and give their opinions, he came up with this perfect joke:

"Did you hear about the two older ladies driving down the street? They ran a red light.

The passenger, Louise, was worried about Myrtle's driving, but she didn't say anything. They then ran another red light, and Louise thought maybe she should say something, but she didn't.

Finally, after Myrtle ran the third red light in a row, Louise said, 'Myrtle! What are you doing? You have run three red lights in a row!'

Myrtle replied, 'Well, Louise, I thought you were driving!'"

Once he'd made us all laugh, Gardner would say, "Now that we know who is driving, let's put our heads together and solve this issue."

I admired Gardner's sense of timing. He always seemed to have the perfect story at the perfect moment. I've never had that mastery. The biggest laughs I get are usually those that come by accident—and are at my own expense. For some reason, this seems to happen most often when we are on family vacations.

Seven members of our family were visiting the Czech Republic, and as we walked through downtown Prague enjoying the beautiful architecture, I ran smack dab into a post in the sidewalk. It was only about three and a half feet tall, and I hadn't seen it because I was looking up at the scenery. I hit the post straight on. Then I went down as if someone had opened a trapdoor beneath my feet.

I was hurting. The members of my family were not sympathetic. Instead, they were beside themselves with laughter. I couldn't get mad at them because it must have looked pretty funny to see me just collapse like that. So I laughed with them until we all cried.

More than 10 years have passed since I Czech-ed out in the Czech Republic, but my family members still enjoy warning me to watch for deadly Prague posts whenever we go for a walk.

The ability to laugh at yourself may be the most beneficial form of humor, and I've certainly had ample opportunity to do that. Given its many positive benefits, laughing easily and often is an extraordinary force for good. A strong sense of humor can help you reduce stress, overcome challenges, strengthen relationships, and enhance your physical and emotional health. Humor gets you to a better place—one where you can see the world from a more relaxed, healthy, positive, enjoyable, and balanced perspective.

Cultivate laughter and a tasteful sense of humor. Have fun. Laugh with friends. Tell jokes. See if you can change stressful, counterproductive situations into happier, more positive situations through appropriate humor.

Self-deprecating humor is a wonderful tool for relaxing people and engaging them. Let go of defensiveness. Express your true, best, good-natured feelings. All of these behaviors can lead to greater peace.

The third step is simple, but it's very important to your well-being. Now let's look at the fourth.

See Yourself in a Positive Light

This is really about being as good a friend to yourself as you are to others. One of the greatest ways for you to find or maintain peace and balance is to accept yourself, love yourself, and see yourself in a positive light. This isn't about being complacent or ignoring your flaws or deficiencies. You should always strive to become your best, and that requires seeking new levels of awareness, empathy, and accomplishment throughout your life.

Often, we are negatively programmed by the influences around us from the time we are young. Studies have found, in fact, that for most people, 70 percent of their thoughts are negative. Too often, our thoughts about ourselves are negative and self-defeating. There are proven methods for replacing thoughts that can hinder your success with thoughts that can empower you.

Once things are right in your mind, you are much more likely to be highly effective in your ventures and relationships. Accept that you can't always be perfect. Forgive yourself for mistakes and failures; commit to learning from them and moving forward. Know that you were put on this earth for a purpose. There is a fine balance between staying motivated to do better and being so self-critical that you become immobilized. So here are a couple of powerful tools to help you stay focused on the positive aspects of your life: self-affirmation and positive self-talk.

"Indeed, the major obstacle to you
achieving the outcomes that you hope
for in life are your thoughts."

—Viktor Frankl

Practice Self-Affirmation

Your subconscious mind can store millions of thoughts and ideas, but the conscious mind can think only *one single thought* at a time. Remarkably, you can choose which thoughts influence your actions. You're probably familiar with the adage, "As a man thinketh, so is he." Your thoughts affect your decisions, and your decisions determine the quality of your life.

I enjoy the way Gandhi phrased it: "Man often becomes what he believes himself to be. . . . If I have the belief that I can do [a certain thing], I shall surely acquire the capacity to do it even if I may not have it at the beginning."

A self-affirmation is a positive, uplifting phrase that you can repeat to yourself throughout the day—I recommend doing so at least 20 times daily—for encouragement and self-motivation. When you use self-affirmation, you teach your conscious mind to focus on that phrase and that mentality.

I Am Kind, I Am Smart, I Am Beautiful

I believe in the power of self-affirmation. We've seen it work in our own family many times, even with the grandchildren. One of our sons decided to test the power of self-affirmation on his eight-year-old daughter, Bella.

One day, while they were driving in the car, my son told her: "Bella, say the words *I am smart*."

"Well, dad, I'm not smart; I'm dumb," she retorted.

He was shocked. Up to that point, he had assumed that his healthy, smart, and lively daughter was brimming with confidence. She earned straight As, and her teachers loved her.

My son was taken aback, so he reassured her: "You are not dumb. You are smart. You are capable of many great things."

Then he asked her to say *I am beautiful.*

To his dismay, she responded: "But, Dad, I'm not beautiful; I'm ugly."

This concerned him, of course, so he would sit down with Bella to practice self-affirmations each day that would build her confidence and improve her self-image. For about a month, he had Bella repeat several statements each night for several minutes: "I am kind. I am smart. I am beautiful."

After four weeks of this, he asked Bella to say these things, and she responded confidently and without hesitation: "I am kind. I am smart. I am beautiful!" Even better, Bella began teaching her younger sister to use the same statements because they had helped her so much.

Our son's work as a parent continues, of course. He regularly reminds all his children of the importance of self-affirmation. He knows that it's easy for teens especially to be influenced by negative and self-defeating thoughts. Bullies, frustration, stereotypes, and negative media can affect us all, so it's important that we keep positive thoughts in mind.

So, how does this idea of self-affirmation apply to you? Consider this question: What is a simple, positive statement you could repeat that would inspire and motivate you—a statement that affirms the best in you? You may be able to come up with a statement quickly, or it might take you several days. Once you've identified an appropriate statement, repeat it aloud at least 20 times a day, and the world will conspire to help you make it a reality. In fact, 100 percent of the people I know who have done this have seen positive results flow in various aspects of their lives.

Practice Positive Self-Talk

Positive self-talk is a close cousin to self-affirmation. This tool helps you feel the way you want to feel. It's also useful for reducing stress and finding peace even in the middle of mayhem and chaos. These simple tools can be powerful if you put your faith in them. Give them a try while keeping an open mind.

You can control your response to feelings; you are the captain of your emotions. When you choose your responses carefully, you establish a level of control that allows you to become your best in everything you do.

One of my companies hired college students as sales staff each summer. The young people went through sales training before being dispatched to cities across the United States. Sometimes we had as many as 700 sales reps in a conference room. It was a fun and energetic environment. One of the things we had our sales reps do during their training was to stand up and enthusiastically repeat the sentence, "I feel healthy, I feel happy, and I feel terrific!" They would say this three times while pumping their arms in the air.

Every time the sales reps got up and did this, it energized the room. It was fun and exciting. The room came alive with positive energy, and almost everyone had a big smile. If you are going to work in sales, you can't be self-conscious and stressed out. You have to be positive and enthusiastic, or your customers are likely to run from you.

The same is true of almost any social situation. Positive people put out positive energy and draw others to them. No one wants to work or hang out with negative, critical, and complaining people. This exercise is a great one for breaking out of negative moods and shifting into a more upbeat attitude.

When I feel angry or upset, I do the same exercise we taught our sales reps: "I feel healthy, I feel happy, and I feel terrific!" I may still feel grumpy or down after repeating that sentence just once, but there's no way I can still feel like the Grinch if I repeat it 10 or 20 times in a row. I challenge you to try. You may feel silly, but that's better than feeling like a pile of dirt, right?

Anger, frustration, bitterness, and self-pity can't stand up against the positive energy you create when you verbalize good feelings and focus your mind on the upside. Bad things happen;

there's no doubt about it. But every day is a gift, so make the most of your time on this earth. It's okay to feel sad and grieve at the appropriate times, but there is little to gain by dwelling on that sadness.

Your mind and body can feel only what you allow them to feel. If you dwell on the negative and bitter, then those feelings will persist. Take charge. Replace those feelings by putting positive words out into the world.

Live in Peace and Balance

We've put some great new tools into your tool box. Self-affirmations can be pulled out and said aloud every day. Positive self-talk works well in specific situations as a self-coaching method when you feel that your attitude needs a tune-up.

The great philosopher Ralph Waldo Emerson knew the importance of remaining in control of your emotions and balanced in your way of life. "For every minute you remain angry, you give up sixty seconds of peace of mind," he said. You can use these simple tools to be more successful in every aspect of your work and your relationships. As a review, I've provided you with several powerful ways to stay on track to becoming your best.

1. Increase balance in your life.

2. Increase your peace through meditation.

3. Laugh often.

4. See yourself in a positive light through self-affirmation and positive self-talk.

As I look back on my life, I see that when I've been at peace in my mind and heart, my relationships and my leadership abilities have been at their best. The confidence of having that balance inside makes it easier for me to reach out and find ways to help others. As Mother Teresa said, "Peace begins with a smile."

You can choose your response to emotions by infusing each day with positive thoughts so that your moods and your attitudes are more conducive to a constructive and accomplished life. These are the things that highly successful leaders do.

Viktor Frankl was spot on when he said: "Indeed, the major obstacle to you achieving the outcomes that you hope for in life are your thoughts." You are the master of your fate. Finding peace and balance during the journey, both personally and in your organization, leads to greater health and happiness and an increased capacity to sustain excellence and fulfillment.

Leadership Action Steps

1. Manage stress by getting to a more peaceful place. Even though you may live in a stressful world, carry your own peace within you.

2. Use the Circle of Peace and Balance to assess how balanced you are in your life. Make adjustments where necessary so that you don't burn out.

3. Evaluate your balance regularly. Evaluate where you are today, and work to maintain balanced growth in your life. Strive to be a well-rounded and whole person.

4. Find inner peace and strength through meditation. Whether it's a few minutes or an hour, use this powerful tool to reduce stress and increase your focus.

5. Chair fly before an important meeting, call, or discussion.

6. When you feel task-saturated, step back, refocus, recalibrate, and then reengage.

7. Laughter and a sense of humor are great medicine.

8. Control the conversation in your conscious mind. Choose a self-affirmation phrase that works for you and then repeat it 20 or more times a day.

9. When you feel down, angry, or discouraged, repeat to yourself this statement: "I feel healthy, I feel happy, and I feel terrific!" You have the power to control your feelings.

CHAPTER 12

Never Give Up!

Persist—and you will succeed.

Never give up is a pivotal guiding constant. If you master all the other principles, but you give up at some point during your journey, you may fail to reach your destination. If, on the other hand, you choose to never give up, you have a much better chance to succeed. You may still have to make corrections in your course, but as long as you refuse to give up, your goals will be within reach.

The key is that you persevere, making corrections or adjustments when necessary, but never giving up. Confucius said, "Our greatest glory is not in never falling, but in rising every time we fall."

Everyone who dares to dream will be tested. Challenges and adversities will appear, often when you least expect them. Maybe your challenge will be a significant financial issue, addiction, the loss of a loved one, a health issue, a natural disaster, or a tragedy like a fire in your home. The point is that everyone will face hard times or opposition at some point. Nobody is exempt from life's challenges.

How will you respond when these challenges come? Will they defeat you, or will you find a way to persevere and find success? The average person has been told no—or that his targeted goals are unattainable—about 148,000 times by the age of 18. Is it any wonder that successful people put aside a no and continue to go?

I hope that by the time you have completed this book, you will have everything that you need if you are to persevere and overcome your failures and other challenges, whatever they may be. You will also need to have mastery over the doubts and self-defeating thoughts that come from within.

Did you know that in the sales world, 90 percent of salespeople, on average, give up after *four* unsuccessful contacts? Yet 80 percent of sales are made after *five* contacts. What's the difference between the highly successful salespeople and those who gave up? It's the will to be politely persistent despite the challenges and rejection. If you're in a sales organization, imagine the difference just *one* more contact will make. Many salespeople give up too soon!

Your unconscious mind is constantly being programmed by the information it receives. Sometimes, despite your best efforts, negative thoughts and attitudes are part of that programming. You may be influenced by the things that you see and hear on television, on newsstands, at the movies, or in the world around you. One of the common negative attitudes and perceptions that you can unconsciously allow to govern your thoughts is that failure is unacceptable.

Sadly, too many people see any failure as final and simply give up trying to achieve whatever goal they'd been seeking. That's just wrong. In fact, it is tragic because many successful people I know have experienced failure, and if they'd given up, they would never have enjoyed the successes they've achieved.

You should never seek failure, but you should never fear it, either. If you do, you'll be afraid to dream, to keep trying, to move out of your comfort zone and toward the career, relationships, and life that you want.

Virtually everyone will experience a failure or setback at some point. As a matter of fact, according to our research, high achievers typically experience at least three to four major failures and seven major successes in their careers. Every highly successful leader who I know or who I have studied has failed—not once, but many times. Consider your own life. How many failures have you had, and how did those help you to succeed later in your life? We can learn great lessons from our own failures and from the failures of others.

If I were to ask you to name the opposite of success, you might well answer "failure." But on many levels, that wouldn't be correct. The real opposite of success is giving up. Consider this: Is failure really the opposite of success? Or is failure a prerequisite for success? Failure that is anticipated, imagined, or experienced firsthand can serve as a step on the ladder to success.

What's the difference between those who succeed and those who never reach their goals? Successful men and women learn from their failures and keep striving to achieve their goals. They may have to adjust and adapt, but they never give up. Instead, they go over, under, and around any obstacles to reach their desired destination or dream. When we persevere and make course adjustments despite failures and setbacks, we are far more likely to ultimately succeed.

> "All endeavor calls for the ability
> to tramp the last mile,
> shape the last plan, endure the last hours toil.
> The fight to the finish spirit is the one . . .
> characteristic we must possess
> if we are to face the future as finishers."
> —Henry David Thoreau

For many people, in fact, failures and setbacks teach them, motivate them, and inspire them to achieve success beyond anything they had imagined. My son David offered me a very personal example of this when he was a young man fresh out of college and just six weeks away from beginning law school. Like many young people, he enjoyed skateboarding, and one afternoon, he and his brother Rob were in the mountains near our family cabin enjoying the challenges of skateboarding and four-wheeling in the rugged terrain. David was on a long board, and Rob was following him on the four-wheeler down a road that was so steep that he hit a speed of nearly 30 miles per hour. That was too fast for him to stay in control, so David decided to slow his board and jump off to avoid a worse crash.

Unfortunately, when he leaped off the skateboard, David's momentum carried him over a 15-foot embankment that he hadn't seen. He hit the ground hard and kept rolling because of the steep incline. Rob raced to help him, but David rolled more than 60 feet down the hill before he stopped.

Rob found him sprawled on the ground and in pain. When he put his hands under his brother to try to lift him, David cried out in pain. Rob wisely laid him back down and called for help.

An ambulance took David to the hospital, and we followed. That evening, I was with David's wife when the doctors brought out his x-rays. We both went weak in the knees when the doctors showed us four clean breaks on his C1 and C2 vertebrae. Our hearts sank as the doctor described just how serious these injuries were: "About 90 percent of the people with these types of breaks either die or remain paralyzed for the rest of their lives."

We held onto hope as the surgeons took over. They placed bolts into his head to anchor a "halo" brace that would keep his neck still while the broken vertebrae healed. The brace prevented him from turning his head, driving a vehicle, or doing most routine tasks. He was in constant pain, and there were doubts that he would ever regain normal functions. As you can imagine, it was a difficult time for him and for all of us who loved him. With the deadline for the start of law school looming, David considered dropping out for a year. He was required to sit motionless with the awkward halo screwed into his skull.

To add insult to injury, he wasn't allowed to shower for three months because doctors feared that water would damage his equipment.

David was feeling ugly, smelly, and awkward, and he was in no mood to start law school. It seemed wise for him to at least sit out for a year and hope that his body would recover so that he could go ahead with law school. If that didn't happen, he thought, it might be better for him to find a career that didn't require so many more years of education.

The other alternative that David considered was to start school regardless of the severe pain and discomfort. He figured that he could push through the first three months (until his head-gear was removed), hoping that his classmates would ignore the fact that he was ugly, smelly, and awkward.

After careful consideration, David went with the more challenging option: to go ahead and begin law school despite his injuries and his ongoing physical therapy. David has always had a quiet "I'll show you" attitude, and in this case, his determination reaped dividends. He refused to give in or give up. He did not allow his injury to hold him back. He started law school on time, graduated with high honors three years later, and was esteemed by all his peers and professors. David is now legal counsel and chief engineer for one of our companies. He and his wife have smart and beautiful children and a great life.

David's decision to start law school on time despite his circumstances is a wonderful example of the pivotal nature of persistence. When I say persistence, I mean the resolve to continue trying to achieve your goals despite opposition, challenges, or failures. Thankfully, David chose to push on with a positive attitude and a vision that no one could shatter. His experience embodies the principle never give up.

How much do you value someone who has the focus, the desire, and the determination to carry on in difficult or trying situations? How can *you* model those same attributes in your own life by being a person who is reliably persistent?

Three Keys to Never Giving Up

There are three steps to help bolster your determination and inspire you to keep striving to achieve your dreams and goals, no matter what opposition, challenges, or failures you experience.

1. Defeat the enemy within through hard work and action.

2. See the value of failure.

3. Hold to a purpose that inspires you.

Defeat the Enemy Within Through Hard Work and Action

Most of the time, who is the greatest enemy you face? It's *you*!

It's not your competition. It's not someone else. It's usually the insecurities and self-doubts that are hovering between your ears. Too often, we serve as our own biggest critics and doubters. I love what Zig Ziglar use to say about this: "We need to get rid of Stinkin' Thinkin'."

We all have to overcome the negative thoughts and self-criticism that spring up just when we need a boost of confidence instead. As a young businessman, I acquired a printing and publishing company. For the first decade, we experienced great success; however, because of some significant miscalculations, the business then began to have a difficult time financially, and we lost millions of dollars within the short span of a few months.

I struggled to figure out how to meet the payroll. There were many nights when I lay awake trying to figure out how to meet our various obligations. For nearly a year, dark thoughts and discouragement kept me tossing and turning: "There's no way I can pay these people back! How can I ever get out of this?"

As I saw it, I had only two options: to walk away from this overwhelming situation or to go to bat and satisfy every financial obligation the company had, no matter how long it took. I experienced an internal struggle, but finally I decided to face the stiff wind and do what it took to satisfy each obligation over the next seven years. There were still times when I had a strong desire to move out of the state and change my name. In the end, though, my conscience and my principles wouldn't allow me to do that. People had trusted me. I was determined to honor and reward their trust.

It became clear that I must take charge of my attitude and my focus and positively go to work. I must be resolute. By replacing negative thoughts of self-doubt with positive thoughts of hope and action, I chose to stand up and face the music. I chose not to give time or sway to the negative voices, but to go on the offensive with a vision, a plan, and action.

My decision to persevere at that early stage in life prepared me for even greater success and happiness down the road. Because I did not give up, I was able to maintain positive and healthy relationships with creditors and other people who realized that I was trustworthy. I have reaped immeasurable rewards as a result.

More important, I am confident of my inner strength and my ability to overcome setbacks by moving forward with hope toward positive outcomes.

I ended up in a better place than I could have ever imagined or hoped for. Although it was a tough period of my life, I'll always be grateful for those lessons.

Work Works

Author J. K. Rowling's personal story may be even better than the fiction she has crafted in her Harry Potter series. In her own inspiring tale, Rowling's hero and her antagonist are the same person. She has often admitted that she had to vanquish the foe within her before she could conquer failure and find success.

Seven years after graduating from Exeter University in England, Rowling referred to her life as "the biggest failure I knew." She was a single mother with a failed marriage. She was jobless, and she was struggling to care for her child. While writing her first book, Rowling battled severe depression and suicidal thoughts. She applied for welfare. She was as poor as anyone could be without being homeless. She had to fend off her abusive ex-husband with restraining orders while trying to write and take care of her daughter in a hostile environment.

At that point, Rowling considered herself a "worthless failure." To make matters worse, the first 12 publishers who read her initial Harry Potter manuscript rejected it. Rowling has said, however, that the opinion of an eight-year-old reader helped shore up her self-confidence and her belief in the series she wanted to write.

The daughter of the chairman of Bloomsbury Publishing in London read that manuscript and demanded that her father give her the next part of the story. She may be the reason that her father agreed to a limited printing of the book. With its release, Rowling began to see herself as a *published* author instead of a failed author.

The first printing was only one thousand copies, but acclaim quickly followed and her career was launched. Once her confidence was boosted, Rowling focused on her writing and flourished. The last book of the series, *Harry Potter and the Deathly Hallows*, sold 11 million copies on the first day of release. Hundreds of millions of devoted Harry Potter fans have viewed the movie version of the books. Today, her Harry Potter brand, which includes books, movies, toys, games, and other lucrative products, is valued at more than $15 billion.

Each time I hear the story of J. K, Rowling, I feel inspired to press on toward my dreams and goals. It's worth noting that one of the inner enemies we all have to wrestle with is the fact that there are no shortcuts to success. Hard work is always required. J. K. Rowling spent many long, lonely hours at the keyboard writing her lengthy and complex novels. Work is often not fun, but if you are willing to do whatever is necessary, it usually wins the day.

We don't always enjoy the discipline that is required, but the rewards of achievement, happiness and joy, ultimately come through work. Whatever your goals and dreams may be, you will have to work for them. Consider it a privilege to have that opportunity. Take joy in your work, and it will take you far.

During my third year in college, I had a summer job at the Southwestern Company, based in Nashville. I sold educational books and Bible dictionaries in Aberdeen, Maryland. Yes, I was a door-to-door salesman! This was truly the school of hard knocks. After a one-week sales training program in Nashville, I headed to Maryland and hit the streets.

My first day on the job was a Saturday. I started at 8 a.m., just as I had been taught in sales school. I was scared to death because my first house was on a country road and it didn't seem like very friendly country. My first knock brought this reply: "What the hell do you want?"

"Nothing," I shouted before hustling on down the road.

The next house I approached seemed to be occupied by ferocious barking dogs. I didn't dare go to the front door, so I stood on the sidewalk and clapped my hands (which is what people do in South America in place of knocking on the door). I felt like an idiot. I probably looked like one, too.

Eventually a woman came out, and after I explained what I was selling, she actually let me into her house. At first I was afraid that she might feed me to her dogs, but they proved to be barkers, not biters. The woman was very kind and receptive to my sales pitch. She bought a set of books!

I'd only visited two houses. I'd been on the street just one hour. My career was launched! I got out my calculator and figured that if I kept on at this pace, I'd earn $16,000 in commissions by the end of the summer (not bad for the early 1970s).

It didn't work out quite like that. I peaked too soon.

I sold nothing for the next two days. My future earnings calculations dropped to $334 for the entire summer. But I kept at it, and my hard work slogging from door to door eventually paid off.

I hit my stride, and I hit my goal of making enough money to pay my tuition and expenses for the following year in college.

I learned that if I just kept working, putting one foot in front of the other, learning from mistakes, and fighting through the nos, I would eventually get enough yeses! As a matter of fact, I learned that the more nos I got, the more yeses I also got, and I made more money. I discovered that the harder I worked, the better I did. This was one of the greatest lessons I've learned.

I actually made it a game to see how many nos I could get and tried to figure out how to have fun being a failure. The more I failed, the better I did if I kept working hard despite the failures or nos. By the end of the summer, I was getting a lot of yeses!

The next summer, building upon these principles, I became a manager and made four times the money. The summer after that, I made five times as much.

I learned a great deal in the door-to-door sales business. In fact, my experiences dealing directly with customers gave me the confidence to buy my first company. I learned that hard work pays off. I also learned that one great way to quiet the self-doubts and negative thoughts is to just roll up your sleeves and get to work.

You may have experienced failure, rejection, or great challenges in the pursuit of your own dreams, but if you refuse to give up on them and do the work that is required, you too may reap rewards beyond any that you could imagine. All you have to do is fight your way through doubts, fears, and debilitating dark thoughts.

Think now of a time or an experience when you just wanted to give up and quit. When you remember that time, how do you feel? How did it affect your life? The next time you find yourself in a challenging situation, take a moment to step back from your negative feelings. Make the decision to reject them, and then to encourage yourself with more positive thoughts and actions. Take a calming positive breath and say to yourself, "I can do this, and I will. It is my nature to never give up."

You can defeat negative internal voices by choosing to tune into empowering thoughts instead. You have the power to decide:

"I will never quit." When those voices come from inside your mind, you can make the decision to cancel them out, stop them, and replace them with self-encouragement and action. Try saying to yourself: "I will persist; I will succeed; I will never give up," and then go to work!

I've seen this happen many times—when you refuse to give up and you take action to pursue your dreams and goals, you create a snowball effect. Allies appear. Doors open. Opportunities arise. The world seems to align in your favor.

> "Nobody wants to see me down
> like I want to see me up!"
>
> —Molly Brown, the famous *Titanic* survivor

If you learn self-control to such an extent that you can adjust your attitude on the run, you will never be defeated by self-doubt, which is the enemy within. Defeating the enemy within through hard work and action is the first of our three keys to the principle *never give up*.

See the Value of Failure

Now, let's look at the second key. Once we defeat the enemy of negative thought, we are empowered to see failure as a learning process rather than a roadblock. When you experience failure, you may be overwhelmed with anxiety and hopelessness. You might even call yourself stupid, blind, or careless. Some people think of failure as a reflection of who they are rather than a result of an unfortunate experience. Self-criticism can be healthy if it is taken in small doses, but you have to counteract it with equal measures of self-forgiveness and determination. Your failures do not define your life unless you allow that to happen.

The healthier alternative is to view each failure as part of a learning process that brings you closer to success. When failure comes, you should view it as an opportunity to look for the valuable lessons. Remember my business setbacks? Some people viewed them as failures, but ultimately they provided me with valuable life lessons that were actually crucial to my later successes.

The following quote reflects lessons learned by someone who was very successful in their field. While reading it, ask yourself what this person did to turn failures into positive learning experiences. You might also want to try to guess who the quote is from.

> "I've missed more than 9,000 shots in my career.
> I have lost almost 300 games. 26 times, I've been
> trusted to take the game winning shot and
> missed. I've failed over and over and over again
> in my life. And that is precisely why I succeed. "

You may have recognized the positive attitude of former NBA star Michael Jordan, the legendary Chicago Bulls guard. As a player, Jordan was a relentless competitor who drove himself and his teammates to six NBA championships.

Despite his intense desire to win, Jordan saw the value of failure. For example, when his opponents began using strong physical tactics to limit his scoring and defense, Jordan learned from his losses. In the next off-season, he undertook a weight-lifting and fitness regimen that quite literally rebuilt his body into one of the strongest in the league. From that point on, Jordan was nearly impossible to stop.

Finding value in loss, failure, and disappointment has been a critical trait of many highly successful leaders throughout history, across all disciplines. The brilliant inventor Thomas Edison, for example, lost years of research and most of his possessions in a fire that destroyed his home. He was 67 years old. His family feared that he would be destroyed by the loss, but the next morning they found him surveying the aftermath of the fire with his spirit undiminished. "There is great value in disaster," he said. "All our mistakes are burned up. Thank God we can start anew."

Within the year, Edison was back on his feet, turning out many of his most important inventions, including the first phonograph that could record and play back sound.

Both Michael Jordan and Thomas Edison were determined to view their failures as valuable assets. Instead of surrendering to negativity and defeat, they chose to reflect upon the opportunities for improvement created by failure and then to try again, all the wiser.

With Jordan and Edison's attitudes in mind, look back at your own life and some of your so-called failures:

- What is one lesson that you have learned from your setbacks?

- How can that lesson help lead you to success?

When a challenge arises, be aware of the words that instinctively come to mind. The thoughts we entertain define our mindset toward failure.

> "You have brains in your head. You have feet in your shoes. You can steer yourself any direction you choose. You're on your own. And you know what you know. And YOU are the one who'll decide where to go."
>
> —Dr. Seuss

If negative, self-accusing, angry thoughts are instinctive to you, then your mindset will be to see failure as worthless. If you choose to entertain positive, self-motivating, and inspiring thoughts, then you're more likely to see failure in a positive light.

In Chapter 10, I invited you to read at least one book a month and to invest 3 percent of your income in your development. You can learn from others and avoid the same pitfalls (like my many years of repaying a debt).

Hold to a Purpose That Inspires You

The third and final key to the principle *never give up* is to hold to an inspiring purpose that can carry you through any situation. This guiding constant came to mind after I read an article in my local newspaper about Chris Williams, who was the victim of a terrible accident.

The Williams family was on its way home when 17-year-old Cameron White, coming from the other direction, slammed into the side of their car. Chris Williams was driving, but he had no time to avoid the oncoming vehicle. The young man who hit them later pleaded guilty to four counts of second-degree felony automobile homicide (charges of driving under the influence of alcohol and leaving the scene of an injury accident were dropped). But before Williams even knew the teenager's name or the circumstances, he knew that he had to "let it go."

He decided to forgive the driver who had caused the accident. Remarkably, Chris Williams made that decision as he stared out his shattered windshield at the overturned car, fully and painfully aware that his wife, their unborn son, their 11-year-old son, and their 9-year-old daughter had all been fatally injured. He and his 6-year-old son survived the crash. Another child, a 14-year-old son, was not in the car that night because he was staying with a friend.

In order to move on and let it go, Chris channeled his grief and energy into helping other victims. He locked on to an inspiring purpose: to save the lives of others and prevent his family from being overwhelmed by despair and anger. Chris even visited the driver of the car that had killed his family members while he was in prison. He recruited that young man to join him in his campaign to stop drunk driving.

What would you do in a similar situation? It is difficult to even consider, isn't it? Would you have the strength to forgive the other driver so that you could rebuild your own life?

We don't ask for adversity or challenges. They often come when we least expect them. Think now about finding a purpose if you should experience a great tragedy. What would drive you to forgive and move on? I'd suggest filing that purpose away for future reference if tragedy should strike in your life. Think about what drives you and tap into it before challenges arise.

Use whatever inspires you as a life vest when storms hit. Cling to your most inspiring visions as sources of strength and determination. The moment you think about giving up, recall what has brought you this far and resolve to continue on toward your dreams and goals.

If you don't have an inspiring purpose that could carry you through serious adversity, I invite you to take a few minutes and determine what could give you the drive and passion to overcome any challenge or hardship. What is your inspiring purpose?

That is the final key to the principle never give up: to persist and to identify and cling to a purpose that inspires you.

Never Give Up

Now, let's review the three keys.

1. Defeat the enemy within through hard work and action. Don't allow destructive voices, yours or others, to hold a place in your mind. Surround yourself with people who encourage you to succeed. Cancel the negative thoughts and allow room for only the positive. Defeat the enemy within through an inspired vision and goals backed up by hard work and action.

2. See the value in failure. Failure is often an important step on the pathway to success. It is simply a rung on the ladder. You should not fear failure. Instead, find ways to learn and grow from it. Celebrate the opportunities provided by failure, even if it's discouraging and disappointing at first. You are at your best when you stand and say, "I can do it better the next time."

3. Hold on to an inspiring purpose, something that will drive you on and help you through any crisis or challenge that might come your way.

Finally, remember that never give up is a guiding constant for successful people, relationships, and organizations. It makes all the difference between those who falter and those who finish.

Your attitude can determine whether or not you will give up when challenges come your way. Resolve now to be strong in challenging times.

William James wrote, "The greatest discovery of my generation is that a human being can alter his life by altering his attitudes of mind. As you think, so shall you be." Your positive attitude, fresh perspective, dynamic spirit, hard work, and willingness to act are your best tools for overcoming obstacles and realizing your dreams.

> "I can choose to rise from the pain and treasure
> the most precious gift I have—life itself."
> —Walter Anderson

Now that you've gone through all 12 principles of highly successful leaders, I invite you to repeat the process of focusing on one guiding constant a week. You can use the blueprint personally, as a family, with a team you coach, and throughout your organization. At the end of the 12-week process, take a week to reflect on, evaluate, and measure how you have done. Look at the progress you've made. How has this progress affected you, your relationships, and your efforts within your organization?

Then, start the process over again. That is the heart, nerve center, and mind of a great and glorious journey. I hope that you enjoyed reading about the guiding constants, and I hope that you will see the end of this book as the beginning of your journey to becoming your best. I wish you well. Always remember that it takes only one person to make a difference!

Leadership Action Steps

1. Defeat the enemy within through a vision, goals, hard work, and action.

2. When you get down, recalibrate and work.

3. Make the law of averages work in your favor. The more failures you experience, the closer you are to a grand success.

4. Lock on to an inspiring purpose that will carry you through the challenges of life when they come. Make course adjustments when necessary, but resolve to never give up.

5. Practice the power of positive thinking. Use only positive language. Eliminate negative language from your vocabulary.

6. Control what you can control. Make a list of what you can control and focus on those items. Refuse to dwell on things that you cannot control.

7. When the going gets tough, the tough get going—endure, persist, and persevere. I will persist. I will succeed.

8. Remember that failure is a rung on the ladder to success. Don't fear it.

9. You are never too young, too old, or too discouraged to give it a shot. Let your motto be: I will never, never give up.

References

All citations are given in order as they appear in the chapter.

Guiding Constant 1: Be True to Character

The story of Gandhi and eating sugar: Craig Schindler and Gary Lapid, *The Great Turning* (Rochester, VT: Bear and Company, 1989), p. 121.

Helen Keller quote on character: John C. Maxwell, *Beyond Talent: Become Someone Who Gets Extraordinary Results* (Nashville, TN: Thomas Nelson, 2011), p. 205.

Polonius to Laertes: *Hamlet*, Act 1, Scene 3, in *The Complete Works of Shakespeare* 11–12 (Philadelphia: George Barrie and Sons, 1899), p. 166.

Jon M. Huntsman quote: Jon M. Huntsman, *Winners Never Cheat: Everyday Values We Learned as Children (But May Have Forgotten)* (Upper Saddle River, NJ: Pearson Education/Prentice Hall, 2005), p. xii.

Guiding Constant 2: Lead with a Vision

Kennedy on choosing to go to the moon: A. E. Cavazos-Gaither, *Gaither's Dictionary of Scientific Quotations* (New York: Springer Science and Business Media, 2012), p. 2330.

Guiding Constant 3: Manage with a Plan

Angela Wolf story: http://www.utexas.edu/features/2005/wolf/index.html.

Foster quote: John C. Maxwell, *Twenty-One Indispensable Qualities of a Leader* (Nashville, TN: Thomas Nelson, 1999), p. 34.

Man's flight through life: Robert Kennedy, *Of Knowledge and Power: The Complexities of National Intelligence* (Westport, CT: Greenwood, Publishing Group, 2008), p. 7.

Goethe quote: Larry Chang, comp., *Wisdom for the Soul: Five Millennia of Prescriptions for Spiritual Healing* (Washington, DC: Gnosophia Publishers, 2006), p. 634.

Jim Collins, *Good to Great* (New York: HarperCollins Business Essentials, 2001), p. 17

Apollo 13 story: Jim Lovell and Jeffrey Kluger, *Apollo 13* (New York: First Mariner Books, 1994), p. 95.

Peter Drucker, *Peter Drucker on the Profession of Management* (Cambridge, MA: Harvard Business School Publishing, 2003), p. 72.

Guiding Constant 4: Prioritize Your Time

Four chaplains on the *Dorchester*: 144 Congressional Record 72 (Washington, DC: U.S. Government Printing Office, biweekly ed., January 27–February 13, 1998), p. 72.

Photos of the four chaplains: http://3.bp.blogspot.com/-LA4BANy1 14k/ToreVDe- ibQI/AAAAAAAACKk/LxkLcOCAQTo/s16 00/4+chaplains.JPG.

Guiding Constant 5: Live the Golden Rule in Business and in Life

Western Oregon sportsmanship: http://www.youtube.com/watch?v =jocw-oD2pgo; also found at http://www.usatoday.com/sports /college/2008-05-01-softball-sportsmanship_N.htm.

Frankl quote: Richard L. Daft and Patricia G. Lane, *The Leadership Experience* (Mason, OH: Thompson-Southwestern, 2008), p. 171.

George Washington's Rules of Civility: Frank E. Grizzard, *George Washington: A Biographical Companion* (Santa Barbara, CA: ABC-CLIO, 2002), p. 363.

Guiding Constant 6: Build and Maintain Trust

Seth Godin blog: http://sethgodin.typepad.com/seths_blog/2007/02 /apologies_ ranke.html.

Stephen M. R. Covey, Rebecca R. Merrill, and Stephen R. Covey, Trust list: Stephen M. R. Covey and Rebecca R. Merrill, *The Speed of Trust* (New York: Free Press, 2006), p. 136.

Ralph Waldo Emerson quote: Emerson, Ralph Waldo, *A Dream Too Wild: Emerson Meditations for Every Day of the Year.* Ed. Barry Maxwell Andrews. (Boston, MA: Skinner House Books, 2003)

Guiding Constant 7: Be an Effective Communicator

M. Scott Peck quote: M. Scott Peck, *The Road Less Traveled: A New Psychology of Love, Traditional Values and Spiritual Growth,* Timeless Edition (New York: Touchstone, 2012), p. 125.

Sue Patton Thoele quote: Sue Patton Thoele, *The Art of Convening: Authentic Engagement in Meetings, Gatherings, and Conversations* (San Francisco: Barrett-Koehler Publishers, 2011), p. 95.

Thomas Gordon story: http://www.gordontraining.com/Hearing _vs_Listening.html.

McCloskey quote: Ralph Keyes, *The Quote Verifier: Who Said What, Where, and When* (New York: St. Martin's Press, 2006), p. 233.

Guiding Constant 8: Innovate Through Imagination

Walt Disney's imagination: http://disney.go.com/disneyinsider /history.

Einstein quote on curiosity: Richard Alan Krieger, *Civilization's Quotations: Life's Ideal* (New York: Algora Publishing, 2002), p. 139.

Number of inventions and patents: "Thomas Alva Edison," *Movers & Shakers: The 100 Most Influential Figures in Modern Business* (New York: Basic Books, 2003), pp. 169–171.

The account of a carbonized bamboo filament: http://www.creativity -portal.com/articles/michael-michalko/creative-thinking-habits -thomas-edison2.html.

Guiding Constant 9: Be Accountable

Dale Carnegie quote on criticism: Dale Carnegie, *How to Win Friends and Influence People* (New York: Simon & Schuster, 1936), pp. 28–29.

Lincoln on commitment: Teresia LaRocque, "Commitment Transforms a Promise into Reality," Erickson Business Center, accessed at erickson.edu in Feb. 2012.

Lee Iacocca quote: Esmonde Holwaty, *Unleash the Billionaire Within: Learn the Mastermind Principle* (Bloomington, IN: AuthorHouse, 2011), p. 348.

The Reverend Will Bowen war on complaining: George Lewis, *Today Show*, NBC, 2007, http://today.msnbc.msn.com.

Guiding Constant 11: Live in Peace and Balance

Zig Ziglar quote: Dan Spainhour, *Coach Yourself: A Motivational Guide for Coaches and Leaders* (Winston-Salem, NC: Educational Coaching and Business Communications, 2007), p. 174.

Gandhi teaching that "Man often becomes what he believes himself to be": Richard L. Deats and Mary Jegen, *Mahatma Gandhi, Nonviolent Liberator: A Biography* (New York: New City Press, 2005), p. 108.

Guiding Constant 12: Never Give Up!

Thoreau quote on enduring toil: J. North Conway, *The Cape Cod Canal: Breaking Through the Bared and Bended Arm* (Charleston, SC: History Press, 2008), p. 74.

J. K. Rowling quotes and story: http://www.facebook.com/pages/J-K-Rowling/ 106783881197?v=info.

Michael Jordan on persistence: M. J. Ryan, *This Year I Will: How to Finally Change a Habit* (New York: Broadway Books/Random House, 2006), p. 63.

Edison quote about fire in lab: Jack Canfield and Mark V. Hansen, *A 3rd Serving of Chicken Soup for the Soul—101 More Stories* (Deerfield Beach, FL: Health Communications, 1996), p. 235.

Dr. Seuss quote: R. A. Wise, *Wise Quotes of Wisdom* (Bloomington, IN: AuthorHouse, 2011), p. 274.

Greatest discovery of my generation: Douglas McGregor, *The Human Side of Enterprise* (New York: McGraw-Hill, 2006), p. xliv.

Index

About the Author

S teve Shallenberger has more than 40 years of experience as a successful business owner, trusted senior executive, professional corporate trainer, and respected community leader. He has lived in Argentina, Uruguay, Paraguay, Mexico, and Spain for over five years doing humanitarian service.

After graduating from Brigham Young University in 1976, Steve launched Eagle Systems International, a global leadership and management consulting firm. He has successfully led companies in three different industries and has a keen understanding of how to thrive in business. During those formative years in his business career, he continued his education at the Harvard Business School. Steve also worked many years with his dear friend Stephen R. Covey. As a key leader, among others, he helped build the world-renowned Covey Leadership Center.

Steve served as president of the Brigham Young University Alumni Association. He was the president of America's Freedom Foundation and he currently serves on their board of trustees. He was a charter member and chair of the Utah chapter of the Young Presidents' Organization (YPO) and is actively involved in the World Presidents' Organization (WPO).

Steve is passionate about his family, having fun, and helping others achieve their potential in life. Steve's success is due to his unique ability to connect with people at personal, interpersonal, and managerial levels in an effective and practical way. He has devoted his life to building people, businesses, and organizations and increasing their prosperity and happiness.

An innovator in leadership and corporate training, Becoming Your Best takes leadership training and team development to a new level using our results-driven success blueprint. It's been 40 years in the making and countless key executives, organizations, athletes, teachers, and individuals worldwide have come to rely on these principles and processes. It's the award-winning training and success blueprint that has been lauded by business leaders around the world because they've finally found a proven program to implement these critical success principles.

Whether in a keynote, seminar, or executive coaching, we give leaders and their teams the tools and know-how to break down performance barriers and be the disruptive company in their industry. When collectively applied, our signature 12 principles will have a profound impact on the revenue, culture, innovation, and productivity of any organization in any industry.

Leadership Tools and Resources

The BYB Store provides leaders with useful tools to use personally or share with their team. From planners to apps, visit the BYB Store today and see what tools will help you.

Motivational Posters

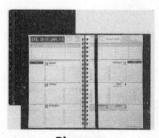

Planners

MP3s

Visit the BYB Store Today

www.Store.BecomingYourBest.com

Motivational Posters, Books, Planners, MP3s, and More.

Take Your Personal Productivity Assessment for <u>FREE</u>!
($97 Value)

In just **6 minutes,** you get a score that tells you how likely you are to succeed over the long-term.

This quick assessment will help you identify specific things you can do to **increase your confidence, focus, and productivity.**

Take Your <u>FREE</u> Personal Productivity Assessment Today!

Visit: www.BecomingYourBest.com